W9-ATP-728

# *Fostering Resilience*

## SECOND EDITION

This book is dedicated to
my grandchildren: Hannah, Avery, Laurel, and Nika.
I hope that I am fostering your resilience.

# *Fostering Resilience*

## Expecting All Students to Use Their Minds and Hearts Well

MARTIN L. KROVETZ

SECOND EDITION

**CORWIN PRESS**
A SAGE Company
Thousand Oaks, CA 91320

Copyright © 2008 by Corwin Press

All rights reserved. When forms and sample documents are included, their use is authorized only by educators, local school sites, and/or noncommercial or nonprofit entities that have purchased the book. Except for that usage, no part of this book may be reproduced or utilized in any form or by any means, electronic or mechanical, including photocopying, recording, or by any information storage and retrieval system, without permission in writing from the publisher.

*For information:*

| | |
|---|---|
| Corwin Press | SAGE India Pvt. Ltd. |
| A SAGE Company | B 1/I 1 Mohan Cooperative |
| 2455 Teller Road | Industrial Area |
| Thousand Oaks, California 91320 | Mathura Road, New Delhi 110 044 |
| www.corwinpress.com | India |
| | |
| SAGE Ltd. | SAGE Asia-Pacific Pte. Ltd. |
| 1 Oliver's Yard | 33 Pekin Street #02-01 |
| 55 City Road | Far East Square |
| London, EC1Y 1SP | Singapore 048763 |
| United Kingdom | |

Printed in the United States of America

*Library of Congress Cataloging-in-Publication Data*

Fostering resilience : expecting all students to use their minds and hearts well / Martin L. Krovetz. — 2nd ed.
   p. cm.
Updated ed. of: Fostering resiliency.
Includes bibliographical references and index.
ISBN 978-1-4129-4958-3 (cloth) — ISBN 978-1-4129-4959-0 (pbk.)
   1. School management and organization—California—Case studies.
2. Resilience (Personality trait)   3. Educational change—California—Case studies.   I. Krovetz, Martin L. Fostering resiliency. II. Title.

LB2805.K688 2008
371.2′009794—dc22                              2007040321

This book is printed on acid-free paper.

07 08 09 10 11 10 9 8 7 6 5 4 3 2 1

| | |
|---|---|
| *Acquisitions Editor:* | Jessica Allan |
| *Editorial Assistant:* | Joanna Coelho |
| *Production Editor:* | Veronica Stapleton |
| *Production:* | Appingo Publishing Services |
| *Cover Designer:* | Tracy Miller |
| *Graphic Designer:* | Monique Hahn |

# Contents

# Preface

Public schooling has changed since the first edition of this book was published in January 1999. Three years later, on January 8, 2002, President Bush signed No Child Left Behind (NCLB). The idea that no child should be left behind is an excellent one. The impact on practice, particularly for schools serving large numbers of students from high-risk environments, has been mixed. On the positive side, NCLB has caused schools to look deeply at the learning needs of individual students. No longer can students of color and English language learning students be excused from high expectations. On the negative side, there are many schools at which students are making large achievement gains, but not large enough to meet the federal NCLB standards. In what way are students at these schools served when their schools are identified as "Program Improvement" and thereby as "failing" within their communities? Many teachers and administrators at these schools feel under siege; many leave the school and/or the profession.

A second change is the opening of charter schools in many communities. The distinction between public and private schooling has become less clear as a result. Charter schools, funded with public monies, are competing with neighborhood and magnet schools for families and for students. When charter schools enroll a student population that is reflective of the diversity in the community, including children of color, English language learners, and special education students, we may learn from these schools. When charter schools enroll a more select group of students or return students to the neighborhood school when they are not performing well or fitting in, the playing field is not level and public schooling is being undermined.

I opened the first edition with the following:

"How do you like my school?" asked María.
"I'm very impressed by how friendly everyone is," said I.
"More important, they really trust me here," said María.

Now more than ever, it is imperative that schools be places where students feel welcome and safe. Of equal importance, students need to feel valued, respected, and known by the adults at the school. Parents, teachers, and administrators need this also. After reading this book, I hope you will be motivated to seek out such schools in your community and work to support the deep commitment and hard work that it takes to sustain them. Truly believing in the potential of all students requires changes in daily practices that are deeply embedded in school culture. This book will encourage you to look at your own deeply held beliefs and offer you tools to examine and redesign the school's culture and practices. It will take considerable skill and courage to lead this effort. Be skillful! Be courageous!

## SEEKING EXEMPLARY SCHOOLS

Initially, Corwin Press asked me to travel and to write about schools that best exemplify fostering resilience for their students. In March 1997 I visited New York City and observed three extraordinary, small, public high schools serving primarily students of color: Vanguard Academy, Urban Academy, and the acclaimed Central Park East Secondary School (CPESS). I also went to New Hampshire to visit Souhegan High School, a very innovative school serving middle- and upper-middle-class students. Several years earlier, on two separate occasions, I had visited Maria's school, South Pointe Elementary School in Dade County, Florida. These are wonderful schools from which we can learn a lot.

Why, however, should you or I have to look far from home to find schools that demonstrate a deep commitment to every student? Such schools should and do exist in every community. The leaders of these schools are courageous and need our voices and support. One of these leaders may be you! Given that school leadership comes from many sources—administrators, teachers, classified staff, parents, students, and community members—reading this book may help you become such a leader.

When I wrote the first edition of *Fostering Resilience: Expecting All Students to Use Their Minds and Hearts Well*, I told the story of seven schools fighting for the hearts and souls of their students. The adults in these schools know their students and their students' work well. They also know their colleagues and their colleagues' work well. As professionals, they accept the responsibility to work with students, parents, the community, and colleagues to create a learning community in which every student is expected and supported to learn. And they come to school knowing how important their work is. All seven schools are within a forty-five-minute drive of my house.

In preparation to write the second edition of this book, I revisited each of the seven schools on several occasions. Some of the schools I was still in close contact with. I made several changes in how I approached the new case studies. First, and of great importance, I know through experience that the theory that school change happens one school at a time is faulty. It is very difficult to sustain change over time without district support. Oak Grove School District truly exemplifies what can happen when a district dedicates itself to closing the achievement gap. Their superintendent, Manny Barbara, is inspirational in his commitment to the education of every child. The new case study in Chapter 2 is about Oak Grove. Rather than update the case study of Stipe, one of the Oak Grove Schools, I have chosen to include case studies of two other Oak Grove schools and how they have been affected by this district commitment.

I wrote in the first edition about my belief in the importance of small schools. In my role as director of the Leading for Equity and Achievement Design Center (LEAD, www.lead-ces.com), a regional center affiliated with the Coalition of Essential Schools (www.essentialschools.org), I have supported the opening of four small schools in our region, all educating students from high-risk environments. The three described in Chapter 5 opened in 2004. The fourth opened in 2006. All are wonderful schools, operating as small schools of choice within existing school districts.

I have updated case studies on Anzar, Rosemary, Chavez, Homestead, and Mission Hill. Moss Land Middle School closed in 2004 and is not included in this edition.

## POTENTIAL OF ALL STUDENTS

*Fostering Resilience* is much more about the passionate belief in the potential of all students and what it takes to foster that potential than it is about particular schools. More than any other single factor, the lack of a deeply held belief in every child's ability leads to students achieving at levels lower than their potential. Most teachers enter the profession believing that every student can be successful, but few experienced teachers hold onto that belief. I do not hold individual teachers or administrators accountable for this. Our society clearly does not believe in the potential of every individual. Our financial priorities as a nation demonstrate our lack of commitment.

At the same time, many of our school practices get in the way. Large schools, large classes, teacher isolation, lack of adequate instructional resources, poorly conceived professional development, inability to stay focused on what is most important . . . these lead to far too many compromises by teachers and administrators, and thereby to a lowering of expectations for students and for themselves. It is not possible for an elementary school teacher, responsible for teaching reading, writing, math, social studies, science, physical education, art, and music to thirty-three students, to demonstrate caring for each of the students. It is not possible for a high school or middle school teacher, responsible for 150 to 200 students, to know each student and the student's work well. It is even harder when multiple languages are spoken by the students, or the societal problems of poverty, drugs, racism, and struggling families impose on the lives of the children and adults in our schools. How can teachers in this situation value the participation of each student? In fact, most teachers welcome students being out sick or cutting classes because the number of bodies is reduced. Most teachers demand that students sit quietly and listen to the teacher talk, because the teacher is overwhelmed by the demands of the job. And yet, there are schools that are working to remove roadblocks to student success.

# RESILIENCE

My vision for the community I want to live and work in is based on fostering resilience, the belief in the ability of every person to overcome adversity if important protective factors are present in that person's life. Resilience is founded on the proposition that if members of your family, community, and/or school care deeply about you, have high expectations and purposeful support for you, and value your participation, you will maintain a faith in the future and can overcome almost any adversity. When the school community works together to foster resilience, a large number of students can overcome great adversity and achieve bright futures.

# THIS IS NOT A SIMPLE FIX!

As you read about the schools featured in this book, you will come to understand the depth of change in school practice and in school culture required to foster resilience for all students. Fostering resilience starts by challenging our underlying beliefs about student potential and how students learn. This strikes at the heart of not only who we are as educators but also who we are as people.

Thus, fostering resilience involves far more than altering the discipline policy, adding social service support to the school, adopting a new curriculum program, buying computers, or having teachers go through a new staff development program. As you read this book, you will come to understand that for a school to attempt to foster resilience for all its students honestly, school practices must be examined. What we teach, how we teach, and how we assess are all central to fostering resilience. How we organize the school and how we group students are central. Likewise, expecting and supporting all students to be literate and to demonstrate the habits of mind to think critically are directly related to fostering resilience.

Fostering resilience serves as a lens to guide school redesign. Look critically at school practices: How does this practice demonstrate caring for every student? How does this practice demonstrate high expectations for every student and support students' efforts to meet these expectations? How does this practice demonstrate valuing student participation?

Focusing my writing on schools is not meant to reduce the important role of family and community.

## ORGANIZATION OF THE BOOK

As you read this book, it will be obvious that I have been heavily influenced by the research of Emmy Werner and the writing of Bonnie Benard. In 1963, Emmy Werner and Ruth Smith began to follow the lives of 614 eight-year-olds, all born in 1955 to plantation workers on the island of Kauai in Hawaii. Werner and Smith have followed these people's lives for over thirty years; one of these people tells her story in Chapter 4. Bonnie Benard has taken the research and translated it into a model that has great relevance for schooling and community development.

In Chapter 1, "What Is This Resilience Stuff?" I present the concept of resilience, summarize Benard's model and Werner and Smith's research, write about gangs as resilient communities, and present Anzar High School—a small, rural, public high school that is demonstrating what can happen when a community believes in the potential of every student—one can eliminate the achievement gap. Within Chapter 1 and continuing throughout the book, I include reflective questions. The influence of this book on your practice will be much greater if you take the time to write brief reflections to these questions as you read. I could have placed the questions at the end of each chapter rather than within; however, I feel that your reflections on these questions are important as you read.

In Chapter 2, "Becoming a Resilient School Community," I present the Oak Grove School District effort for moving schools toward becoming more resilient learning communities. The case study is written by Superintendent Manny Barbara.

In Chapter 3, "What's in It for Me?," I discuss the reasons why a school community should want to foster resilience for its students and staff and what gets in the way. I also present Edenvale and Parkview Schools, two of the schools in Oak Grove. The case studies are written by Ginny Maiwald and Robert Topf, administrators in Oak Grove.

In Chapters 4, 5, and 6, I discuss the protective factors—caring, high expectations and purposeful support, and participation—at the core of fostering resilience. In Chapter 4, "I Care, You Care, We All Care," I update the case studies of Rosemary and Chavez schools. I place them together because their stories are similar, both serve almost entirely English language learners, students at both schools have demonstrated substantial achievement growth over time, and both are identified under NCLB as Program Improvement schools. In Chapter 5, "Providing High Expectations and Purposeful Support," I present Adelante, LUCHA, and Renaissance, three new small schools of choice within the Alum Rock School District. In Chapter 6, "Valuing Meaningful Student Participation," I update the case study for Homestead High School. In each of these three chapters, I offer a brief list of what I look for when visiting a school to determine if the school culture, curriculum, instruction and assessment practices, and roles of teachers and administrators support the fostering of resilience. As you read this book, you will come to understand the depth of change in school practice and school culture required to foster resilience for all students.

The primary purpose of this book is to help school leaders understand and apply the concept of resilience as a guide for proactive, systemic school redesign. The first six chapters should give the reader a sense of how schools that are fostering resilience look, sound, feel, taste, and smell in practice. Systemic change is not exportable, however. Experience and research clearly tell us that one cannot take what one school or district is doing, bring it unchanged to another school or district, and see the concept implemented and sustained successfully. The writing of William Bridges (1991) has been a major influence on my thinking. Change is external; transition is the internal process every person goes through to adjust to the external change. Leading and managing school change is really about caring, high expectations and purposeful support, and valued participation that is carefully planned and orchestrated to help every individual transition. Chapter 7, "Managing Change," discusses how schools and people change and updates the story of Mission Hill Middle School.

You will have many questions about fostering resilience and implications for schooling. In Chapter 8, I present my top-ten list of commonly asked questions about resilience, along with my answers.

## 15,000 HOURS—DOES IT MATTER WHICH SCHOOL A CHILD ATTENDS?

Children spend approximately 15,000 hours in K–12 schooling. Michael Rutter (1979) asked whether a child's experiences at school have any effect. Does it matter which school the student attends? These questions led Rutter to study twelve inner-city London secondary schools in depth. He used four measures of student outcomes: attendance, pupil behavior, examination success, and delinquency. His research indicates that the school attended does make a difference. He found that schools differ markedly in the behavior and attainment shown by their pupils, and schools that performed better on one of the four student outcomes generally performed better on the others.

## CAUTION: RESILIENCE IS A RELATIVE TERM

Few people make it through childhood, adolescence, and adulthood without many ups and downs. Everyone experiences periods of serious suffering. As Weissbourd (1996) writes, "Children described as resilient are often simply children who have not yet encountered an environment that triggers their vulnerabilities" (p. 40). Nothing is fixed. Children who are in trouble at one point in their lives often right themselves at some later point. In fact, it is difficult to predict which children in high school will thrive as adults. Often, those selected as most popular or most likely to succeed in high school struggle as adults, whereas others who struggled socially as teenagers appear to adapt very successfully as adults.

## A FINAL NOTE

It is November 8, 1996. I am sitting in a bakery in Berkeley, California, with Emmy Werner. We have not met before. I am telling her about my ideas for this book. She immediately offers two challenges:

1. "Beware of how you use the term *resiliency*. It is being abused by people seeking grant money. It has been used by both Clinton and Dole in the recent election campaign. The cover story for the most recent *U.S. News and World Report* (Shapiro, Friedman, Meyer, & Loftus, 1996) is on resilience. There is even a brand of panty hose and a face cream called Resilience."

2. "Please, please, please, do not write a testimonial to schools you like. Demonstrate that these schools are affecting student outcomes in positive ways."

This book is neither a longitudinal study like Emmy Werner's, nor a quantitative study like Michael Rutter's. In response to Emmy's challenge, however, I do include student achievement data at the end of each case study that indicates that these schools are having a positive influence on the learning of children.

When presenting this data, I use the Academic Performance Index (API): California's accountability requirements, reported in terms of API criteria, measure the academic success of a school on the basis of how much it improves annually. Schools have a minimum growth target for the school year, and the target varies according to the API score at the beginning of the year (API Base). The growth in a school's API reflects the progress that school made from one year to the next (http://www.cde.ca.gov/ta/ac/ap/documents/infoguide05g.pdf). I chose to not use the NCLB criteria Adequate Yearly Progress (AYP) as the primary achievement criteria. API indicates growth over time, value-added. AYP is criteria-based and has goals for all schools to reach that are raised over time such that all students should demonstrate proficiency by 2014.

# Acknowledgments

This book has been largely inspired by the research of Emmy Werner and the writing of Bonnie Benard. The concept of resilience is the focus of my teaching and work with schools in the community largely due to how clearly the idea of fostering resilience speaks to the reasons why I am an educator. I am also inspired by the dedicated teachers and administrators I work with and know in the public schools in our region. To the teachers and administrators working to foster resilience in our schools, stay courageous!

I want to thank the following people for their input into the revised lists of what to look for when visiting schools: Paula Arnold, Cathy Jo Diaz, and Ann Kenny. I also want to thank Bonnie Benard and Sara Truebridge for their time and feedback.

To Marsha Speck, my colleague and friend and with whom I developed the school change model presented in Chapter 2, our work together is our legacy. To Pat Stelwagon and Dennis Chaconas, my colleagues in the LEAD Center, our work together motivates me to take retirement only half seriously.

To my wife Judy, my children Marc, Ted, and Emily, their spouses Zhong Lin, Emma, and Ken, and my grandchildren Hannah, Avery, Laurel, and Nika, I hope that I am helping to foster your resilience. You are at the core of my resilient community.

To Rachel Livsey and Phyllis Cappello at Corwin Press, thanks for your faith in my writing.

To longtime friends and family, read about yourselves in Chapter 1. I appreciate the lifetime of fostering resilience that we have given each other.

Corwin Press wishes to thank the following peer reviewers for their editorial insight and guidance:

James R. Bean
Professor of Leadership Studies
Psychology Department
Lock Haven University
Lock Haven, PA

Bonnie Benard
Senior Program Associate
WestEd
Oakland, CA

Mark P. Boggie
ASCA Western Region VP
Cochise Community College
Sierra Vista, AZ

Kathy Gomez
Director, Educational Services
Evergreen School District
San Jose, CA

Jerry Patterson
Professor, Educational Leadership
University of Alabama at Birmingham
Birmingham, AL

Kate Thomsen
Educational Consultant, Facilitator, Author
Private Practice and Associate with Heart of Change
Syracuse, NY

Sara Truebridge
Research Associate
WestEd
Oakland, CA

# About the Author

 **Martin L. Krovetz,** PhD, is the director of the Leading For Equity and Achievement Design Center (LEAD), a regional center of the Coalition of Essential Schools. From 1991 to 2006 he was a professor of educational leadership at San Jose State University. During this time, he developed and coordinated the master's in collaborative leadership program. From 1977 to 1991 he was a high school principal in Santa Cruz, California.

In addition to being the author of the *Fostering Resillience*, he is the author with Gilberto Arriaza of *Collaborative Teacher Leadership: How Teachers Can Foster Equitable Schools*, published by Corwin Press in 2006. He has been published in numerous journals and presents at national conferences, including ASCD and the Coalition of Essential Schools.

He received his PhD in social psychology from the University of North Carolina and BA from the University of Florida. He can be reached at mkrovetz@email.sjsu.edu.

CHAPTER ONE

# Whatever Happened to That Old Gang of Mine?

" Can our students really meet our expectations for each of the six exhibitions for graduation?"

"Well, whom are you concerned about?"

"How about Jill? She is a special education student."

"I work with Jill every day. She is doing well in all of her classes. She is coachable and is motivated. She will be intimidated at first, and she'll need extra help, but if her advisor and I work closely with her, she'll pass all exhibitions."

"How about Louisa? Her English language skills are still weak."

"We've already agreed that students can do the oral part of the exhibitions in their primary language as long as they do a major part of one in a second language. Louisa can choose to present in Spanish as long as one substantial presentation is in English. We have a rubric in place for second language."

"You're right. Louisa will do fine."

"How about Jack?"

"Jack is my advisee. We all know him well. He is lazy and a behavior problem, but capable. We will work with him and with his parents. Hopefully, he'll choose to take this seriously in order to graduate. If he does, he'll do fine!"

This discussion and others like it take place regularly at Anzar High School. Anzar is a small, rural high school, founded on the principles of the Coalition of Essential Schools (CES). Due to its small size and its commitment to a strong student advisory program, teachers know all students well. Conversations like this occur often and typically involve the entire staff. The conversation you just read included comments from six teachers. The case study at the end of this chapter describes the school in more detail.

Unfortunately, few teachers and administrators know their students and their capabilities as well as the staff at Anzar. However, within most communities you should be able to find an Anzar, a Rosemary, a Cesar Chavez, a LUCHA, a Renaissance, an Adelante, an Edenvale, a Parkview, a Homestead, or a Mission Hill. Hopefully, after reading this book, you will—as a teacher, an administrator, a

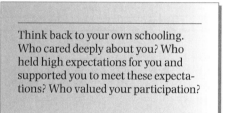

Think back to your own schooling. Who cared deeply about you? Who held high expectations for you and supported you to meet these expectations? Who valued your participation?

parent, a community member, a student, a staff member, a grandparent, or school board member—seek out such schools in your community and work to support the deep commitment and hard work that it takes to sustain them. You will hopefully ask why every school is not more like these schools and help remove the obstacles for schools that are striving to be "resilient learning communities." At the same time, you will better understand how hard it is for these schools to stay resilient for all students when faced with the accountability challenges of No Child Left Behind (NCLB).

## DEFINITIONS

**Resilience**—the ability to bounce back successfully despite exposure to severe risks (Benard, 1993, p. 44).

**Resilient community**—a community that is focused on the protective factors that foster resilience for its members: (1) caring, (2) high expectations and purposeful support, and (3) ongoing opportunities for meaningful participation.

Schools are often faced with many obstacles that hinder their ability to support resilience. Most schools and most classes are too large and the school day is too harried for teachers or administrators to know each student well and therefore to care deeply about him or her, set high expectations, offer purposeful support, and value the participation of each student.

You, the reader, are urged to stop and write a brief response to all or most of the questions posed in this book. Even if you take just a few seconds to answer each question, you will find this book to be much more useful.

## WHATEVER HAPPENED TO THAT OLD GANG OF MINE?

As reflected in Abe Maslow's famous hierarchy of needs, all people seek out love and belonging. All people want to know that others care about them, have high expectations for them, and will support them to meet the expectations, and want their voices to be valued. All people seek out groups of people who will foster their resilience. AND these groups come in all sizes, shapes, and forms. My "gang" was a group of friends with whom I walked home from school, played ball at the corner playground, and went with to synagogue, boy scouts, camp, and 88th Street Beach. They were the friends I played with when our parents socialized together. These friends—my gang—were a very positive force in my life.

My other "gang" was my extended family. We spent every Sunday at my grandparent's house, so did my aunts, uncles, and cousins. I was the oldest grandchild, and the only male for many years. I received incredible love, attention, and validation. My family made it clear to me that their expectations were high—the family carpeting store was named Benmor, not Benmor and Son. My father and mother were clear with me—I was to go to college and do something important with my life. It was also made clear to me that, as the oldest, I had certain responsibilities to "be a good boy, a mensch" and to lead by example. I was lucky. My gangs provided a positive resilient community for me.

When I finished my PhD, I moved to California, far from family and friends. I married a woman from Iowa who was divorced with two young sons. We found that the family gang did not exist for us or for our children; family and old friends were too far away. The gang for our children (we added a daughter to the world in 1973) became little league, softball, swimming, water polo, music, and scouts. Yes, needless to say, athletic teams, performing arts, and scouting groups are positive forms of gangs. In fact, these constructive activities and "gangs" offer similar attractions: sense of purpose, a hierarchical system of discipline, and a chance to prove loyalty to a group. In all likelihood, when you think positively about your school experiences, you think of relationships that resulted from your involvement in these types of activities.

## WHATEVER HAPPENED TO THAT OLD GANG OF THEIRS?

Children have a need for social affiliation and, in most cases, choose peer relationships that are constructive rather than destructive. Richard Weissbourd (1996) writes that children's

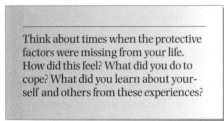

Think about times when the protective factors were missing from your life. How did this feel? What did you do to cope? What did you learn about yourself and others from these experiences?

peer groups tend to become destructive when children lack a basic ingredient for healthy growth: positive sources of recognition, especially meaningful opportunities that extend into relations with adults. Children have to believe that they can create a better life. If they have this belief, they will strive. Without the perception of meaningful opportunities, children have less reason to be afraid of the repercussions of their destructive behavior.

As a high school principal, I always advised new students to be involved in some positive aspect of the school, one in which they could make friends and receive positive adult attention easily. I suggested they become involved in the choir, the band, the school newspaper, athletics, or the student council. Without this positive connection, new students would find the students on the fringes of the campus much more open to making new friends than the students already involved in positive ways within the school community. For many years, I initiated and facilitated a school service club, one of the primary functions of which was to welcome other students into constructive activities at the school.

Shame is very common among adolescents and younger children. Weissbourd discusses research with prison inmates indicating that many criminals were chronically humiliated in their youth. In my experience, many high school students do not feel valued and feel shame in the school setting. Often this occurs in one or more of the following three areas:

- Classroom
  Many students find classroom learning irrelevant to their lives, and whereas many alienated students are behind in their academic skills, primarily reading skills, they are gifted students bored by the lock-step nature of classes. They feel shamed by their teachers for not doing homework or performing well and by their poor grades, so they attend school less and less regularly.

- Physical Education
  Whereas some alienated students are not athletic, many are excellent athletes; in my community, they are often surfers and skateboarders. They dislike the competitive nature of physical education classes and are shamed by teachers and peers for not caring about winning. They dislike the special status given to the school "jocks." They stop dressing out and stop attending.

- Peers
  In any school, it is clear which groups are "in" and which groups are "out." The in-group usually occupies a central place in the school, physically as well as status-wise. Many alienated students feel hatred and shame when in contact with the in-group of a school. They will not walk in certain areas of campus, feel lack of ownership with and connection to the school, and attend less and less regularly.

For several years while I was the principal of Soquel High School, we offered an afterschool opportunity class for ninth and tenth graders who were not attending school regularly. These students were told not to be on campus until two o'clock daily and to attend school from two to five o'clock. These "non-attendees" came to school every afternoon on time. They talked with the teacher and with me about how, for the first time, they felt connected to the school. The students who had disrespected them had already left for the day. They attended classes with students like themselves and were connected to an adult who cared about them, had high expectations for them, supported them, and valued them. I didn't know at the time that these were resilience factors. I viewed the school differently because of these conversations.

## MOVING FROM RISK TO RESILIENCE

> In every child who is born, under no matter what circumstances, and no matter what parents, the potentiality of the human race is born again.
>
> —Agee & Evans, 1960, p. 289

Practitioners in the social and behavioral sciences often follow a problem-focused "hospital model" to try to address the needs of at-risk people. A problem focus involves identifying the risk factors—dysfunctional family, disease, illness, maladaption, incompetence, or deviance—and seeking resources to develop programs to work with at-risk populations. This approach is reactive in that programs are designed to help people who are already identified as being in trouble. In schools, many alternative programs are designed for these populations. Staff members can place students who are behind academically in special education classes or in Title 1 classes. They can place truant and behavior-problem students in in-house detention centers, opportunity classes, independent study, and continuation schools.

The problem-focus model offers little help to educational and community leaders who would prefer a more proactive position. These leaders would prefer to build communities based primarily on protective factors that would reduce the need for special programs for at-risk students because fewer students would be at risk. A proactive position is based on building capacities, skills, and assets—building resilience. It emphasizes strengthening the environment, not fixing kids. In fact, we should use the phrase "students from high-risk environments" rather than "at-risk students," since being proactive means impacting the environment, not defining the child.

## WHAT IS THIS RESILIENCE STUFF?

Based on longitudinal studies, researchers have found that for every child coming from an at-risk background who later needs intervention, there is a higher percentage of children who come from the same background who become healthy, competent adults. Werner and Smith's definitive research that serves as the foundation for resilience theory (RT) is described in more detail in Figure 1.1.

> Talk with someone who overcame great adversity. To what or whom does this person attribute his or her success? What did this person do to cope? What did he or she learn about him- or herself and others from these experiences?

RT is based on defining the protective factors within the family, school, and community that exist for the successful child or adolescent—the resilient child or adolescent—that are missing from the family, school, and community of the child or adolescent who later receives intervention (Benard, 1991; Speck & Krovetz, 1995). Werner and Smith (1992) write that the resilient child is one "who loves well, works well, plays well, and expects well" (p. 192).

Resilient children usually have four attributes in common (Benard, 1991, 1993, 1995):

- **Social competence** (ability to elicit positive responses from others, thus establishing positive relationships with both adults and peers)
- **Problem-solving skills** (planning that facilitates seeing oneself in control and resourcefulness in seeking help from others)
- **Autonomy** (sense of one's own identity and an ability to act independently and exert some control over one's environment)
- **Sense of purpose and future** (goals, educational aspirations, persistence, hopefulness, and a sense of a bright future)

Most people have these four attributes to some extent. Whether or not these attributes are strong enough within the individual to help that person bounce back from adversity is dependent on having certain protective factors in one's life. The

---

**Figure 1.1**    The Definitive Research: Emmy Werner and Ruth Smith's Longitudinal Study

---

*Fostering resiliency isn't just putting stuff into an empty box by the teacher, or elder, or whatever else. It's based on countless interactions between the individual child or adolescent or adult and the opportunities (in their) world and the challenges they face.*

—Werner, 1996, p. 21

In 1963 Emmy Werner and Ruth Smith began following the lives of 614 eight-year-olds, all born in 1955 on the island of Kauai. For the most part these children were Japanese, Filipino, and part or full Hawaiians. Their parents came from Southeast Asia to work on the sugar and pineapple plantations on the island. Most were raised by parents who were semi- or unskilled laborers and who had not graduated from high school. The primary goal of this longitudinal study was to assess the long-term consequences of prenatal complications and adverse rearing conditions on the individual's development and adaptation to life. The story of these children is told in Werner and Smith's (1992) book *Overcoming the Odds: High Risk From Birth to Adulthood.*

As Werner and Smith report, the majority of the children were born without complications. However, one-third encountered four or more risk factors before the age of two. Two out of three of this latter group subsequently developed serious learning and/or behavior problems by age ten or had a record of delinquencies, mental health problems, or pregnancies by age eighteen. Nevertheless, one out of three of these high-risk children had developed into competent, confident, and caring young adults by age eighteen. Quite impressively, by age thirty-two, two-thirds of the remaining at-risk group were functioning satisfactorily. Assessment of functioning satisfactorily was based on individuals' own accounts of success and satisfaction with work, family, and social life, and state of psychological well-being, and on their records within the community. For the follow-up at age thirty-two, data for 505 of the original 614 individuals was secured.

Highlights of relevant findings:

- 40 percent of the resilient group had at least some college, compared to approximately 17 percent of the total population studied and 13 percent of the cohort with long-term coping problems.

---

**Figure 1.1** *(continued)*

---

- Most of the resilient children had at least competence in reading skills; Werner and Smith emphasize the importance of this finding for educators, adding that effective reading skills by grade four was one of the most potent predictors of successful adult adaptation.
- Most of the resilient males came from households where there was structure and rules and had males who served as role models.
- Most of the resilient females came from households that emphasized risk taking and independence, with reliable support from female caregivers.
- For both resilient males and females, their ability to recruit substitute parents was a major feature of how they differed from those found not to be as resilient. These substitute parents unconditionally accepted them as they were.
- Resilient children often were pressed into having to care for younger or older family members. This "required helpfulness" seems to carry over into their adult lives.
- Resilient children had faith that life would work out and a belief that life made sense; this may or may not be linked with organized religion.
- Resilient children were good at making and keeping a few good friends.
- Resilient children took pleasure in interests and hobbies that allowed them to be part of a cooperative enterprise.
- Resilient adults remember one or two teachers who made a difference for them.
- Nowhere were the differences between the resilient individuals and their peers more apparent than in the goals they had set for themselves. Career and job success was the highest priority on the agenda of the resilient men and women, but the lowest priority for their peers with problems in adolescence.

A more recent follow-up at age forty, confirms these findings.

Excerpts from "The Faces of Resiliency" by Mervlyn Kitashima (1997), one of the participants in Emmy Werner and Ruth Smith's study, is included as Figure 4.1.

---

following are key protective factors needed within the family, school, and community:

- **A caring environment**—at least one adult who knows the child well and cares deeply about the well-being of that child (Chapter 4)

- **Positive expectations**—high, clearly articulated expectations for each child and the purposeful support necessary to meet these expectations (Chapter 5)
- **Participation**—meaningful involvement and responsibility (Chapter 6)

## DOES THE PRESENCE OF THESE PROTECTIVE FACTORS RELATE TO STUDENT LEARNING?

WestEd conducted a comprehensive, longitudinal study (Hanson, Austin, & Lee-Bayha, et.al., 2004) examining how gains in NCLB test scores are related to health-related barriers to student learning. Results indicate a significant relationship between test score gains with each of the following: caring relationships at school, high expectations at school, and meaningful participation in community. Results also showed a significant negative relationship between gains in test scores and reported sadness/hopelessness. The study found no significant differences related to whether the schools were low or high performing. Does the presence of these protective factors relate to student learning? Clearly, YES!

## WHERE DO WE GO FROM HERE?

Fostering resilience in children is a long-term project involving systemic change within the communities of children. It isn't something we do to kids. It isn't a curriculum we teach to kids. It isn't something added to a school or community with short-term grant money.

Supporting resilience in children is based on deeply held beliefs that what we do every day around children makes a difference in their lives. It is about dedicating our hearts and minds to creating communities that are rich in caring, high expectations, and purposeful support, and opportunities for meaningful participation. It is the understanding that the culture and daily practices of schools need to be redesigned in ways that demonstrate a deep commitment to the potential of all students, and it is the courage to work to create such schools.

As our social institutions have fallen apart—no need to outline here the effects of divorce, mobility, long work hours, poverty, racism, sexism, and so forth on our children and on society—more and more is expected of schools to meet the social and psychological needs of students. At the same time, people constantly criticize schools for not preparing graduates with the academic skills to be productive members of the American workforce. In response to a multitude of conflicting demands, many schools lack clarity of focus, offering a program that resembles a shopping mall—lots of independent shops in which browsing is encouraged and buying is optional (Powell, Farrar, & Cohen, 1985).

> Think about three students who you know well and who are different from each other. What does their school do to foster resilience for each of these students? Specifically, what do people at their school do to help each of them feel cared for, know that expectations are high and support is strong, and know that their participation in the life of the school and classroom is valued? What do each of these students need in order to experience a more resilient learning community at their school? Use these students as a lens as you continue reading this book and as you look at your school.

## Special Note

Some researchers differentiate between "resilience," which is the dynamic process of competence despite adversity and "resiliency," which is a specific personality trait (Luthar, 2000). In this book, I try to use the words in this way. The Luthar article is an excellent review of the theoretical framework for research on RT.

# CASE STUDY: ANZAR HIGH SCHOOL

## Written Spring 1998

Merrill Vargo, director of the Bay Area School Reform Collaborative (Hewlett-Annenberg school reform initiative), has said to me on several occasions that one of her fondest hopes for school reform is that there will be at least one high school in Northern California that people view as an exemplary model as they do Central Park East (CPESS) in New York. I have told her that Anzar will be that high school.

## A School Snapshot

At a staff meeting during the spring of 1997, we made a list of students who might be in need of additional support. We listed sixty students who fell into one or more of the following categories: special education, English learning, migrant, attendance, behavior, and grades. We quickly eliminated approximately twenty names because they were doing well in school. An individual plan was set and implemented for each of the other students. Many had or would have a community mentor to help them with their school studies, to support them in preparing for their graduation exhibitions, or to offer

> Yet, there are schools—the rare schools that exist in each of our communities—that maintain high academic standards and at the same time serve as resilient communities for children and adults. The schools presented in this book are fighting for the hearts and souls of their students. They are places where students feel trusted, accepted, supported, and respected. They are places where adults know students and their work well.

them a career apprenticeship. I know of no other high school where this quality of student focus occurs. When students are known well, they do not "fall through the cracks." Some students may not be as academically successful as we would like, but every student is treated respectfully, and no student is written off or forgotten.

## Background Information

Anzar High School is a new, small, rural high school located in San Juan Bautista, a mission town south of Silicon Valley. All students work closely with a teacher-advisor throughout their four-year high school career. The relationship that develops allows Anzar to implement two important programs: service learning and graduation by exhibition. The school is teacher led; there are no administrators or guidance counselors. Anzar is a member of the Coalition of Essential Schools.

My involvement with the Aromas/San Juan Unified School District began in 1991. The Aromas/San Juan Unified School

District arose from a grassroots, unification effort initiated by parents seeking student-centered, community-oriented schooling for their children. As part of a unification vote in 1990, a school board was elected to oversee the formation of a new school district and to develop a high school to service the two communities. Previously, Aromas School was part of a large K–12 school district, which has its own comprehensive high schools. San Juan was a single K–8 school, which fed into a neighboring, large comprehensive high school. One of the new board members enrolled in the Educational Administration Program at San Jose State University and was a student in the first class I taught there. We quickly recognized the common vision we had for the schools, and I was hired to facilitate the search for the new superintendent. I have stayed involved with the district as a critical friend for the new superintendent, both for K–8 schools and for Anzar High School. Three of the initial four high school teachers were teachers I had worked with while principal of Soquel High School, approximately forty miles away.

High school classes began in the fall of 1994 with approximately 60 ninth-grade students. An additional 40 students joined Anzar High School in 1995, another 50 in 1996, and another 120 in 1997. It is expected that the school will grow to approximately 450 students in Grades nine through twelve by the year 2000. These students represent a multicultural population (40 percent Hispanic; 50 percent white, not Hispanic; 10 percent other). The clientele includes special education, fluent-English-proficient, limited-English-proficient, non-English-proficient, Title 1, and gifted students.

For its first three years, Anzar met in temporary buildings on the Gavilan Community College campus. The new high school facility did not open until the fall of 1997. During this time, many of the students took college classes for credit. Students continue to do so, particularly for advanced placement course work. Gavilan is approximately five miles from the new campus.

## Uniqueness of the School

We know everyone. We know teachers inside out. They are on a first-name basis with you. It isn't by second semester that they are getting to know you; it happens by the second day, or third day max.

—Anzar senior

Anzar is a special place for students and adults. The smallness of the school and the commitment to a student advisory program means that every student is known well by several adults. The conversation at the beginning of this chapter really is a regular form of conversation at Anzar. I have never been in a school that so consistently makes decisions and has discussions in which the appropriateness of action is so centered on what is best for individual students. Parent and student voices are also important in decision making. In fact, and very unique to this school district, one high school student is elected at Anzar to be a voting member of the school board; on several occasions the student's vote has been the deciding vote on important issues.

In talking with several teachers about how to best present Anzar, we agreed that I should present four important components of the school. We feel that these components demonstrate the uniqueness of the school and are at the core of how Anzar provides the protective factors that foster resilience for its students.

### Everyone Agrees on the Givens

Because the school is new, its culture is being defined every day. However, staff, students, and parents have taken the time to agree on the "givens" for the school (see Figure 1.2). The givens are the principles that the school is based on and that are no longer up for grabs. These principles guide our practice when tough decisions need to be made. When new teachers are hired, we expect that they will come to Anzar because they want to work at a school that is based on these principles. Teachers may not always be sure how to challenge students to use their minds well, develop exhibitions, design curriculum where depth of coverage is stressed over breadth, coach rather than tell, integrate curriculum, and so forth, but they chose Anzar and Anzar chose them because of their desire to be a part of this special school. The teaching staff is truly outstanding! And yet, school life is never easy. One of the givens is the commitment to full inclusion and to heterogeneous grouping of students. Given the wide breadth of student academic background, teachers struggle every day with meeting students' needs. They talk regularly about modifying curriculum for special education students and about expectations for English learning students. They talk regularly about how to motivate and support students who can't or won't read and, at the same time, how to challenge motivated students. Several teachers mention feeling overwhelmed by the demands of differentiating instruction for so many of their students. More students fail classes than we would like. And it is hard to find enough time to collaborate on these issues. Teachers often wonder aloud, **"Can I handle it here?" "Is it worth it?"**

*Graduation Is by Exhibition*

To graduate from Anzar all students must prepare and present six exhibitions: math, language arts, science, social science, service learning, and post graduate plans. These exhibitions are in addition to more traditional course requirements. The rubric for the exhibitions is based on the "habits of mind" we expect our students to develop. We call our habits EPERRs (evidence, perspective, extension, relevance, reflection; see Figure 1.3). Students often wonder aloud, **"Can I handle it here?"** The following student comments in bold print indicate that, although "stressed to the max," students recognize the value of the Anzar experience.

These exhibitions are intended to be centered on issues/questions of importance to students that are complex enough for them to explore from multiple perspectives. Students are encouraged to use an interdisciplinary approach and therefore to combine more than one exhibition at a time. All exhibitions have an oral and written component. Since we value the arts and require some second-language proficiency for all students, students are required to integrate both of these into at least one of their exhibitions. Exhibitions are judged by community members who volunteer their time for this purpose. Students know the value of this work: **"At first, one of the hard parts is to take a general subject like math or science and put it into a real-life situation, where if you were just studying out of a textbook you wouldn't know the difference."**

---

**Figure 1.2**　　Anzar's Givens

---

1. Community
   Service learning
   Responsiveness to the community
   Community/student input
2. Inclusion
   No tracking
   All children can learn
3. Professionalism
   Site-based management
   Teachers as administrators
   Teachers planning/teaching together
   Communications guidelines
   Collegiality
   Teachers as learners
4. Quality
   Integrated curriculum
   Small class size
   Depth over breadth
   Advisory
5. (High) Expectations
   Graduation exhibitions
   Lifelong learners
   Ability to use EPERR

---

I have judged exhibitions ranging in topic from capital punishment, to the relationship of favorite music, to how students dress, to why the guitar is the most influential instrument of the twentieth century, to why science fiction literature is more than entertainment, to setting up an afterschool sports program for one of the local K–8 schools as a service-learning project. I observed exhibitions almost totally in English by two bilingual Latinas, one presented on bilingual education and the other on why Mexicans are not welcome in California. I judged a math exhibition done by a Latino student who has been in the United States for only two and one-half years, done totally in English, about the influence of population growth in China; he was able to answer my questions about linear and multiple regression. I judged an exhibition entitled "Is Tree Farming Sustainable in the Future?" that counted for language arts, social studies, math, and science, and deservedly so.

**Figure 1.3** Habits of Mind—Anzar's EPERRs

**Evidence: What do I know and how do I know it?**
What are all the choices?
Show the evidence.

**Perspective: What are the biases—mine and others?**
What do I already know from my past experiences, and what's my bias?
What is the bias of the research used?
What are alternative points of view?
What did I learn from the experiences of others?
Walk in somebody else's shoes.

**Extension: What are the deeper implications?**
How might this affect the future?
What if something changed?
Is there a pattern here?
How does this connect to other ideas/issues?
Going beyond what you know . . .

**Relevance: What difference does this make?**
Why is this important to me?
How can I use this?
How does this issue influence the community?
How is this important to my community?
What can people do with this information?

**Reflection: What did I learn?**
What other questions does this bring up?
Has what I've done changed my way of thinking?

One of the wonderful benefits of exhibitions is that a student receives very specific and primarily positive feedback, recognition, and praise from the judging panel, as well as constructive criticism as to how the exhibition could have been stronger. One student said to me, **"You get a real sense of accomplishment when you do the first one. You read about exhibitions, and like it's impossible, but when you do it and pass it, it's like I did it and didn't think I could."**

Students compare their high school experience to those of friends at other high schools and say, **"Our school has a very high bar for achievement that requires that you be on top of things. There is no way to get out of things. There is no way to skate**

**through the system."** One of the main complaints I hear from students is that they do not have a laid-back senior year.

Be clear—exhibitions are very different from a senior project. Senior projects usually are a research project done in a special class taken during one semester of the senior year; school practices need not be impacted. Exhibitions and our EPERRs are the guiding principles for instructional and student assessment practices throughout the school. All teachers are expected to develop curriculum and to utilize instructional and student assessment practices that prepare students for their exhibitions. Every class is affected.

Of course, a commitment of this magnitude impacts the work life of the teachers. A few teachers are given the class assignment of coaching students for their exhibitions. However, when the coach is an English teacher, the student and coach spend considerable time with the math teacher, for example, working on the math exhibition. The time involved is considerable and a necessity if the student is to be supported to do quality work. In addition, the time to coordinate exhibitions—judge recruitment, judge training, copying student written work for the judges, coaching, setting up the rooms, buying refreshments, entering exhibition results on transcripts, maintaining a written and video library of all exhibitions, etc.—all takes time outside of the regular expectations for teaching. Teachers wonder aloud, **"Can I handle it here?" "Is it worth it?"**

*The School Is Teacher Led*

The school employs no administrator. Currently, three teachers are elected each year and given release time to serve as the leadership team. No one may serve for more than two consecutive years, and leaders must teach for at least 60 percent of the day. The school has hired a classified office manager to oversee many of the management functions of the school. The leadership team makes most schoolwide decisions in a weekly staff meeting by consensus. As a result, teachers feel full ownership and responsibility for decisions made. Many parents and students also feel ownership due to their involvement in school committees, and, for students, based on schoolwide discussions held in advisories (see Barnett, McKowen, & Bloom, 1998).

Students have spoken with me about the advantages of a teacher-led school. They feel that this encourages teachers to act as a whole. No one authority figure "rules over" the students. And because of the responsibility all teachers have for the success of students and the school, teachers know students better and value their input.

Advisors are the primary contact with and for parents regarding any and all issues affecting students, including school progress, discipline, and post-high school planning. Currently, advisor responsibilities come on top of teaching five classes. We have been unable to figure out a practical way to make advisory part of the regular assignment and still maintain reasonable class sizes. Again, teachers regularly wonder, **"Can I handle it here?" "Is it worth it?"**

The governance structure also impacts parents—they are not always sure who to go to for answers to their questions, and they are used to being able to go to "the principal" when they want an issue addressed. The role of the superintendent is also different. He is the primary evaluator of all Anzar staff. Unique to Anzar, the teacher-leadership team, with union approval, participates in the evaluation of all probationary teachers. The superintendent also sits in on many leadership team and staff meetings and knows the school much better than the superintendents of most school districts.

### *Time for Planning Is Built Into the School Calendar*

Being part of Anzar can be a burnout job, and we grapple constantly with how to support the resilience of the adults. We know that time is the most precious resource to support teacher and school renewal, and we have built in time in several ways for this reason.

Students leave campus an hour and a half early every Wednesday. Staff meetings take place during this time and almost always end at 3:30. In addition, the David and Lucille Packard Foundation and the Walter S. Johnson Foundation have provided money for twenty paid planning days, used primarily in the summer, for all staff to collaborate on refining the exhibition process, curriculum development, and other issues of importance to the school. These days are in addition to the eight professional development days provided by the state and approved by the school district. There is never enough time, but at least the staff knows that, as professionals, they have time weekly and in the summer time to be reflective and collaborative.

## Another School Snapshot: The Students' Point of View

I am sitting with eight seniors. I have told them about my book and have asked them to talk about how Anzar has fulfilled their expectations or not done so. This is Anzar's first senior class. These eight, along with about thirty-five of their friends, have been the oldest students in the school for their entire high school careers— as they said to me, **"We have been seniors for four years."**

They spoke warmly about the high expectations and support they receive from teachers and each had stories to tell. One of the students had left Anzar for her sophomore year to go to a large high school and had returned. She talked about how at the large high school teachers and counselors did not know her, yet told her what to do. At Anzar, **"Teachers take the time to know me well, to give me choices, and to support the choices I make."** She also spoke about how at the larger high school, which was 90 percent Latino, she felt that discrimination occurred toward Latinos in terms of school expectations and among Latino students themselves. At Anzar she said that each student is seen as an individual and all students get along. She summed up her thoughts: **"At the large high school, teachers are committed to their jobs. At Anzar they are committed to students."**

The students spoke at length about how the graduation exhibitions set "a high bar" that all students are expected to meet. It is February and only one of the eight has finished all six exhibitions; she is the only student in the school to have finished. They talked about "feeling cheated" because they are not able to coast during their last semester as their friends at other high schools were doing, and of the stress related to making post-high school plans, finishing required course work, and preparing exhibitions. They spoke of how exhibitions taught them how to set goals and meet them; to research, write, speak, and coordinate information; to see how school content relates to real life; to research things other than what teachers teach; to use the Internet; to interview experts; to use several libraries; and to work independently with the teacher as a guide. They talked about the pride and sense of accomplishment they feel as they present their exhibitions, and of their responsibility to be role models to help younger students appreciate the value of the exhibitions and the commitment it takes to do them well.

They also talked about how the smallness of the school brought students together—no cliques, no in-groups or out-groups; they are all friends. They felt relatively safe from violence, gangs, and drugs. One student said, **"The change from junior high school to high school was easy because there were no big classes, and we didn't get drowned out by the other voices."** They also spoke about missing some of the school activities that exist at the larger high schools—more sports teams and pep rallies. And they spoke about missing Gavilan College, where they had had more freedom of movement, better food services, a library, and full science and art labs.

They talked with me about the advantages of a teacher-led school. One student said, **"I think the standards are higher here because teachers care about us more. Our relationships are so close that they want the best for us."**

Anzar is a resilient learning community. Reading the words of students clearly demonstrates that students know that teachers care about them, that expectations are high, that teachers support them, and that their participation in their learning and in the daily life of the school are valued.

## Update Written Winter 2006–2007

Anzar is thriving. Anzar is a California Distinguished School that has eliminated the achievement gap between Hispanic and white students. Now in its fourteenth year, Anzar is viewed as the school of its community. For the first ten years, some parents and students behaved as if Anzar was a school of choice. When the work became too hard, when college preparation expectations for all students were high, and when students worked on exhibitions as juniors and seniors instead of coasting like their friends at neighboring high schools, some parents and students requested interdistrict transfers. Some people initially viewed Anzar with suspicion. Anzar's lack of a principal, graduation by exhibition, habits of mind, service learning, advisories, and lack of a football team were just too different for some community members to initially trust. No longer!

What changed the perspective? I asked teachers this question in the fall of 2006. Their response was:

- recognition as a California Distinguished School in 2005;
- older siblings and friends graduated from Anzar and were successful in college;
- sports teams being increasingly successful;
- parents recognizing the value of the strong relationships that exist amongst students and teachers, especially tied to the continuing commitment to advisory;
- teachers stay at Anzar; few teachers wonder anymore, "Can I handle it here?" "Is it worth it?";
- Anzar's listening to the parents' desire for a principal and appointing a leader from within the school to serve as principal in 2002.

I am still a critical friend to the high school, but I no longer serve as an official school coach. Sitting and talking with faculty and students is like coming home for me. Please note how clearly the protective factors of resilience are at the heart of this school.

I asked the faculty to tell me what had changed and what had stayed the same since this book originally was published. The first comment from most teachers was that Anzar has a much clearer focus on equity.

## Focus on Equity

In 2002 the district hired Glenn Singleton and the Pacific Education Group to work with teachers at the three schools in the district on issues related to race, equity, and white privilege. Following two days of professional development with all teachers, each school selected a team of teachers to receive more intense professional development and classroom coaching, with the understanding that these teachers would then share their learning with the full staff. Anzar took this very seriously. Six teachers spent the next three years engaging and sharing in this learning.

Look at the following data for Adequate Yearly Progress (AYP), the measure tied to NCLB. For the most recent data, 2005 to 2006, the percentage of students "at or above proficient" in English-Language Arts is basically identical for Hispanic/Latino and white (not of Hispanic origin)students, and Hispanic students performed slightly better than white students in mathematics. **Anzar has eliminated the achievement gap.** Very few high schools can make this claim.

| Percent at or above proficient | | |
|---|---|---|
| | *Hispanic* | *White (not of Hispanic origin)* |
| English-Language Arts | 62.3 | 63.0 |
| Mathematics | 66.7 | 64.8 |

A few teachers admit that initially they considered themselves color-blind and had viewed this as a positive trait. Now, after "staggering" self-examination, and regular in-depth conversations about race, every teacher talks about designing instruction with specific target students in mind and how much their instructional strategies have changed. They also discuss how over time many more Latino students "are into making good grades" and that white students as well as students of color talk about equity and racial awareness. The teachers speak proudly of the schoolwide focus on academic literacy and the recent addition of a math lab to help students fill specific gaps in their math skills while enrolled in the college-prep Algebra class. They talk about how as a faculty and individually they use data for decision making and how target students serve as real people when they plan their lessons. The principal talked with me about pulling back layers and not myth making and **"the more we knew, the more we realized what we were doing wrong."**

Beginning in 2006, the principal decided it was essential to work with eighth-grade Latino students in the two feeder schools as part of a vertical push downward for raised expectations. Once a week for seventy-five minutes, nine Latino high school students go to the two feeder schools and work with Latino eighth-grade students on academic projects. The work is done in Spanish in order to build the academic Spanish literacy of the eighth-grade students and to hopefully give these students a sense of belonging and pride in native language use. This is a powerful way to model for eighth graders that it can be "cool" to be Latino and to be smart and stand out academically.

**The rest of the Anzar update is organized around the four components of the school as described in the original case study.**

## The School Focuses on the Givens

As teachers talked with me about the givens, they focused on five key areas: advisory, communication guidelines, responsiveness to the community, service learning, and inclusion.

- **Advisories** are at the heart of the school. In 1998 many teachers wondered if the extra student load was worth the time and effort, and a few teachers left because of the workload. In 2006 every teacher agreed that the relationships among teachers and students is what makes Anzar special. It is in advisories that "transparent celebrations of achievement" occur and where students help other students with class work, with graduation exhibitions, and with mini-exhibitions at ninth and tenth grade. It is where teachers share themselves with their students, and how over four years strong "family ties"' develop amongst students, parents, and teachers. Over time, much more staff meeting time is being devoted to grade-level planning for advisories.

- **Communication guidelines** have served as the norms for all meetings and, at least as important, for how people have talked with each other for most of the school's fourteen years. Every faculty meeting ends with all participants filling out a written rating for that meeting in comparison to the meeting norms. Every faculty meeting begins with a summary of the ratings from the previous meeting. For me, more impressive is that one communication guideline in particular is followed conscientiously by staff members: **"I talk directly to any person with whom I have an issue in a timely manner."** Several people stressed how important this particular guideline is to maintain the strong collegial relationships that exist at Anzar. One teacher said that the guideline does not make it any easier to have the hard conversations with one's peers, but "at Anzar you just do it." Another teacher commented about how the guidelines not only make him a better colleague, but also a better person away from school.

- **Responsiveness to the community** led to the appointment of Charlene McKowen, one of the original four Anzar teachers, to the principalship in 2002. In addition, at one time there were concerns within segments of the Latino community that the uniqueness of Anzar might not be best for its students. Because of these concerns, the staff had to have difficult discussions with the community and students. These discussions led to the focused commitment to practices that assure equitable learning opportunities for all students.

- **Service learning** continues to be a six-semester graduation requirement and part of one of the graduation exhibitions. Over time, more and more opportunities for service learning are provided on campus—in the community garden, as a peer tutor, and by working at the school/community-sponsored farmers market.

- **Inclusion** continues to be a way of life at Anzar. Teachers are expected to differentiate instruction and accommodate all students, while maintaining high standards for all students. Special education teachers coteach with other teachers and model differentiation.

## Graduation Is by Exhibition

Whereas the exhibition guidelines are reviewed and revised almost every year, student exhibitions still serve as the culmination for all students to demonstrate the quality and depth of their learning at Anzar. The school's habits of mind (EPERRs) continue to serve as the rubric for exhibitions, and their use is deeply engrained in every teacher's instructional strategies. Over time, students have increasingly chosen to do interdisciplinary exhibitions, a goal from the beginning. And, as teachers have learned to teach in ways that are consistent with the school's vision, students post essential questions and teachers use these questions to guide instruction in class. Increasingly, as teachers have learned to assess in ways that are consistent with the school's vision, performance-based, mini-exhibitions turn into graduation exhibitions, a goal from the beginning.

## The School Is Teacher Led

In 2002 Charlene McKowen, one of the original Anzar teachers, was appointed principal. The parents asked for this so that lines of authority were more clearly delineated. In conversations with teachers, they agreed that, whereas Charlene now takes care of many routine matters well, important decisions are still made by consensus (fist of five) at staff meetings. One teacher talked about the importance of leadership coming from within the school, how as a result the school's givens continue to drive decision making, and how everyone continues to share leadership responsibilities. A second teacher discussed how the system capitalizes on the various personalities among the staff and how this leads to everyone having a voice and no one being an agitator.

Allied with these comments, four teachers completed the Urban High School Leadership Program (UHSLP) in 2006. This program, offered by the Educational Leadership Department at San Jose State University, my department, leads to a master's degree and an administrative credential. Enrollment is by school teams. The purpose is to prepare high school leaders to be assistant principals in urban high schools, with a focus on collaborative leadership and the importance of school leaders being skillful at staying focused on issues of equity and closing the achievement gap among its students. The four teachers are engaged in important leadership roles at Anzar. Charlene is an earlier graduate of this program.

## Time for Planning Is Built Into the School Calendar

It is imperative that teachers have concentrated time to reflect on schoolwide and classroom practices. Initially, grant money was secured that paid teachers for twenty workdays each summer. Later, Gates Foundation monies allowed all staff to have some summer paid days. This money has now run out. For many years Anzar staff meetings have been primarily used for planning. This is particularly important now that money for summer planning will be hard to come by. Students leave early on Wednesdays. In a typical month, one Wednesday is used for advisory planning, one for content area planning, one for a schoolwide curricular focus (i.e., literacy or the intersession curriculum), and one for a general meeting or district inservice or not held due to exhibitions, and so forth.

In addition, when the Coalition of Essential Schools Fall Forum (national conference) was held in San Francisco in 2004, the school calendar was arranged so that teacher workdays were scheduled during the conference and all teachers attended.

## Anzar High School
2000 San Juan Highway
San Juan Bautista, CA 95045
408-623-7660
Web site: www.asjusd.k12.ca.us

**Enrollment**: **394**
Hispanic 44.8%
White (not Hispanic) 50.3%

| API | 1999 | 2005 | 2006 | Change |
|---|---|---|---|---|
| Total | 597 | 707 | 729 | +132 |
| Hispanic | 537 | 644 | 690 | +153 |
| White (not Hispanic) | 678 | 757 | 762 | + 84 |

CHAPTER TWO

# Prerequisites

*First Things First*

*Change throughout the system will not come about through a thousand points of lights, but from the steadily increasing, concentrated light and heat of one sun.*

If there is a lesson to be learned from the multitude of school reform initiatives over the years, it is that school change cannot sustain itself one school at a time. The relentless, focused energy needed to reconceptualize our schools in ways that foster resilience for all students requires a systemwide effort of the full school district. The case study in this chapter is about Oak Grove School District and its courageous journey to close the achievement gap. It is written by Manny Barbara, the district superintendent. The case studies in this chapter are about two schools in Oak Grove.

If school professionals do not believe deeply that ***all students can learn to use their minds and hearts well***, little else matters. No professional development program, no new instructional materials, and no infusion of technology will make a lasting impact on student learning if the key adults in the student's life do not believe in the potential of each and every student. When I ask experienced teachers if they believe that all their students can succeed academically, most are unsure or answer in the negative.

When I ask these same teachers to remember their first years as teachers, they clearly remember coming to work with the firm belief that what they did was important, based on the conviction that every one of their students could be increasingly successful in school. Why is it that many teachers lose the sense that what they do every day is important? What can be done so that teachers maintain their sense of purpose?

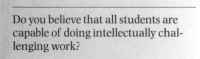

Do you believe that all students are capable of doing intellectually challenging work?

My colleague Marsha Speck and I have developed a model (Figure 2.1) that presents what we think are the prerequisites that must be coming into place to support a school creating the conditions to support student success. Just as "coming" and "creating" end in "-ing," the components of our model are evolving processes that may have a clear beginning, but have no ending.

**Figure 2.1**    Resiliency Model

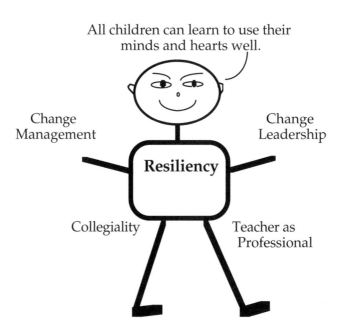

# FIRST THINGS FIRST: THE HEAD

Any effort to improve the quality of life and learning for students must begin with an examination of our underlying beliefs. This requires a much deeper look than the usual efforts to write a school vision statement, by consensus, across various segments of the school community. School leaders need to carefully exam their own underlying beliefs about why they come to work every day and what they believe about students as learners, and then cause their colleagues to undertake the same careful examination. Implicit in this reflection is the collection of data, especially student work, that is examined to learn if student work offers evidence that the beliefs one professes are in fact occurring in practice.

> Think about the three students you reflected on in Chapter 1. Do you believe that each is capable of intellectually challenging work? What evidence do you have? What do you do to challenge each of these students, and how do you support their work?

I have spent time in schools and school districts that have done an excellent job of focusing time and resources on high-quality professional development around instructional strategies, particularly literacy. Test scores typically go up. However, this is not enough. Such initiatives do not require teachers, staff, and administrators to deeply examine their underlying beliefs about children. Focused time and resources also need to go into learning cultural literacy (Lindsay, Robins, & Terrell, 2003) and having the courageous conversations focused on issues of race, ethnicity, gender, language, and socio economic status that will uncover blockages that inhibit high achievement for all students (Henze, Katz, Norte, Sather, & Walker, 2002; Singleton, 2006). This is what happened for teachers at Anzar High School. This is what is happening in Oak Grove School District.

People have asked me what I mean by "using one's mind and heart well." Go back to the Habits of Mind (EPERRs) in Figure 1.3. When students demonstrate that these habits of mind are an integral part of how they think and act, they are demonstrating their ability to use their minds and hearts well.

If school staff say that they believe that all students can use their minds well, then if I visit that school I should see the following evidence:

- lots of student writing based on students thinking about issues that are relevant and important to students;
- teachers using questioning strategies that require all students to think more deeply;
- students at work in classrooms, rather than students listening to teachers working;
- student assessment strategies that evaluate the student's depth of thinking;
- teachers modeling critical thinking through their engagement in action research projects designed to improve their own practice.

If school staff say they believe that all students can learn to use their hearts well, then if I visit that school I should see the following evidence:

- students working cooperatively in groups in which every student is participating, and individual accountability is clear;
- students serving as and receiving peer and cross-age tutoring;
- students engaged in service learning activities;
- students engaged in learning about and contributing to the solution of real issues of concern to the students and to the community;
- teachers modeling by working together as peer coaches and reviewing student work together;
- principals modeling by engaging teachers, students, and parents in meaningful work on school, district, and community issues;
- recognition programs in place that reward cooperative achievements rather than individual achievements.

Please note the depth of change in school practice and in school culture that is required. Fostering resilience is at the core of schooling.

# THE RIGHT LEG: COLLEGIALITY

Schools will not be successful if teacher practice is primarily based on working in isolation from other adults. Teachers need to know each other and each other's work well. Outstanding schools are not composed of 1,000 individual points of light, but instead have a clear beam of powerful, focused light starting from 1,000 sources. Collegiality is discussed in more depth in Chapter 3.

# THE LEFT LEG: PROFESSIONALISM

The redesign of our schools, more than anything else, is a quality of life issue. Teachers and principals need to believe that they are more than *"just teachers"* or *"just school principals."* Teachers and principals need to be seen and recognized as professionals; they need to see themselves and recognize themselves as professionals. They need to believe that what happens inside their classrooms, each and every class period, each and every day, is of critical importance, and just as important is what happens outside of their rooms—in other classrooms and throughout the school— and they need to believe that they can influence what happens inside and outside their rooms. Issues of professionalism are discussed in Chapter 3 as related to intellectual stimulation, respect, voice, and job satisfaction.

# THE ARMS: MANAGING AND LEADING CHANGE

Being part of a school that truly assesses its underlying beliefs, that practices collegiality, that respects employees as professionals, that truly is working to be a resilient learning community, is courageous work. School leaders need to have the skills, knowledge, attitudes, and behaviors to lead this effort. Chapter 7 focuses on change.

# THE HEART: RESILIENCE

Keep reading!!

# CASE STUDY: OAK GROVE SCHOOL DISTRICT

## Closing the Achievement Gap—Everyone Makes a Difference

Over the last nine years, the Oak Grove School District has embarked on a journey to close the achievement gap. The phrase "closing the achievement gap" first appeared in the Oak Grove District in 1998 as part of a systemic approach, involving all stakeholders within the district system, to close the achievement gap among African American/Latino and White/Asian students. The final product was the "CTAG Plan," a plan of action eventually adopted by the board of trustees, which clearly identified this equity issue as our central instructional focus.

## Systems Approach

In a systems approach to improving student performance, everyone plays a role.

Figure 2.2 reflects the dynamics of looking at the district as a system of interrelated factors all playing a role in enhancing the teacher-student interaction. This *Theory of Action* suggests that all district elements are variables impacting student performance. The "district" refers to all components supporting schools (e.g., educational, human resources, business services), with the heart of the instructional process being the teacher-student interaction. Student success occurs districtwide when the instructional process and relationships between teacher and student reflect best practices. Students can be successful within a poor school if an individual teacher is particularly outstanding, just as an individual school can demonstrate outstanding results within a district that may not be especially exemplary. However, if the criteria for success require that all students within all classrooms and all schools are successful, then the district as a system becomes the primary unit of change. Each year I welcome our staff with the same challenge—we do not need test scores to let us know how we are doing. Are we willing to place our own children in any school with any teacher? The answer should be an unqualified "yes!"

**Figure 2.2**    Oak Grove School District (System Theory of Action)

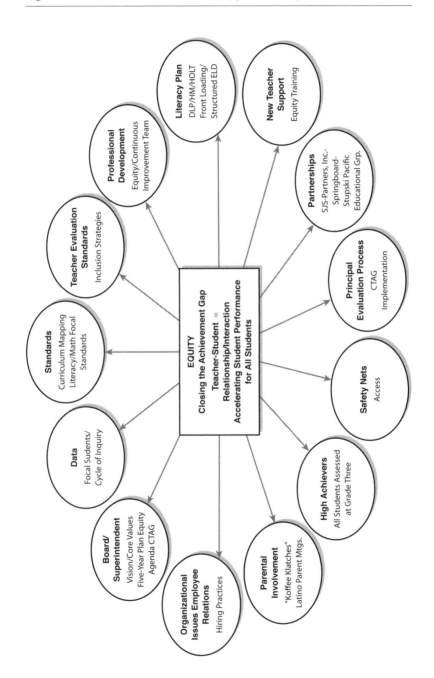

## Role of Superintendent—Board of Trustees

The role of the superintendent is to lead and manage the district system in such a way that the focus is always on the instructional process through the teacher/student relationship. While no aspect of this system is ignored as a variable potentially affecting student performance, no one component is by itself the only factor determining student performance. Arguably each might be weighted differently in the potential impact on student success. For example, if hiring practices are sound, then potential exemplary staff are already in place, requiring less professional development.

One of the most important variables affecting overall district student performance results is the board of trustees–superintendent relationship. If the system as a whole is to be positively impacted, the board and superintendent must agree on district priorities based on a shared district vision and core values, and have a clear understanding of the differences in roles between the governance role of the board of trustees and the leadership responsibilities of the superintendent. In the Oak Grove School District, this is manifested in the "Five-Year Plan," a document outlining the district priorities for the coming year and in the years to come. The "Five-Year Plan" is a collaborative process, including input from all stakeholders, revised and adopted annually, and transparent for all to see. It is posted on the district Web site and discussed annually with each school staff and both district and school parent groups. Detailed action-plan activities pertaining to each priority area are identified as well. It is the superintendent's (and by definition the entire leadership team's) responsibility to implement the activities behind the "Five-Year Plan" priorities. The board of trustees adopts the overall priority areas and holds the superintendent accountable to implement the activities without engaging in micromanaging.

Once the board and superintendent share a vision and priorities, then the challenge is for all within the system to share the vision and focus on the priorities as well. This can be accomplished only through a collaborate process wherein the identification of priorities involves all district stakeholders.

# Equity Lens

The Oak Grove District approach in tackling the achievement gap is comprehensive in nature. All elements are viewed through an equity lens. For example, the district's "Five-Year Plan" clearly identifies closing the achievement gap by accelerating African American and Hispanic student performance as a district priority, giving it status by making it transparent. Furthermore, data is disaggregated in numerous ways (e.g., ethnicity, mobility, focal students). The use of data to drive decision making is key, both at the microclassroom level and the macrodistrict level in delivering needed resources. Both formative and summative data are utilized, while a standards-based delivery system ensures that all students are exposed to and learn state standards. Instructional best practices are continually pursued and generated through ongoing professional development. The "Professional Development Plan" is continually adjusted to reflect new data and a changing workforce with differing needs and sensitivity to the increasing accountability pressures and workload.

Feedback loops are part of the system to allow for input from staff. Two examples are the District Vision Advisory Committee (DVAC) and the Listening Committee. The DVAC consists of the three employee association presidents, the community liaisons, several teacher members at-large selected to reflect existing staff, and the cabinet (lead principals, assistant superintendents, and superintendent). The DVAC meets several times a year as a "climate check" and influences district priorities through input to our ongoing "Five-Year Plan." The Listening Committee consists of teacher members of the District Literacy and Equity Teams. It meets annually with the superintendent and responds to the question, "What do you want us to continue, start, and stop doing?" As a result of input from the Listening Committee process, professional development activities are modified accordingly.

However, closing the achievement gap solely through an instructional focus is not considered sufficient. Once the equity challenge is accepted, the stakes are raised considerably. In pursuing a system's approach to CTAG, *race matters*. Our "critical friends," Glenn Singleton of the Pacific Educational Group, and more recently Edwin Javius of EdEquity, have pushed us to look at all aspects of the system from an equity lens. Once color is acknowledged as a variable where "color blindness" is exposed for what it is—continuing a dominate white culture—then race and the emotional tension that comes with it needs to be addressed. "Courageous conversations," to use Glenn's phrase, can be challenging once racism is confronted. One challenge has been to address the balance between those who see the need to accelerate our efforts and those who feel we are moving too quickly. For people of color especially, we cannot move too quickly to address organizational issues that may sustain the achievement gap, even if done inadvertently and unintentionally.

A critical first step in closing the achievement gap is delineating the difference between equal and equity. "Equity is not a guarantee that all students will succeed. It assures that all students will have the opportunity and support to succeed" (Singleton, 2006). This means that resources are distributed in an equitable manner—to accelerate the performance of African American and Hispanic students—rather than equally distributed in a way that the status quo remains in place.

To mitigate the variability of perceptions, the focus and use of disaggregated data becomes even more important as the benchmark to measure progress. Increased parental involvement through African American parent meetings (called Koffee Klatches) and Hispanic Parent meetings (HABLA) are held at the schools and at the district level. An administrative support group was created called ALLIED (African American and Latino Leaders in Equity Development), sponsored by the superintendent to help retain administrators of color and to give them a voice. Our workforce and especially our leadership team has been diversified.

## Partnerships Help!

Partnerships have played a critical role in helping to move the district agenda forward. Two ongoing partnerships with San Jose State University are the Teacher 20 percent Intern Program and the Master's in Collaborative Leadership Program (MACL). Both help build district capacity, either through recruitment (e.g., intern program) or professional development (e.g., teachers receiving an advanced degree). The 20 percent Intern Program allows future teachers to learn the art and science of teaching while in the classroom of a master teacher while being paid 20 percent of a salary. At the end of the internship year, the teacher can expect to be hired on a full-time basis. MACL has been instrumental in providing a critical mass of staff who have received advanced training in collaborative leadership. Teams of teachers engage in a two-year learning process attending graduate-level classes held within the district, culminating with a master's degree in educational leadership; enrollment is as school teams; learning is very much focused on learning and practicing job-embedded skills, attitudes, and behaviors consistent with the district's CTAG initiative.

All other components in the diagram play a crucial role in promoting student performance and are interrelated. By recognizing this interdependence and intentionally addressing its value, each can have a positive impact on overall student performance.

The Oak Grove School District's *Theory of Action* emphasizes that each member of a school system makes a difference every day, some through direct contact with students, others by ensuring that interaction with students occurs in the best possible manner. The district becomes a primary impetus for transforming practices, acknowledging and working to ensure that each decision and practice accelerates student performance for *all* students.

## Oak Grove School District

6578 Santa Teresa Blvd.
San Jose, CA 95119-1204
408-227-8300
Web site: www.ogsd.k12.ca.us

| **Enrollment**: | **8,295** |
| --- | --- |
| African American | 6.1% |
| Asian | 17.4% |
| Filipino | 3.1% |
| Hispanic | 41.4% |
| White (not Hispanic) | 26.2% |

| API | 2002* | 2005 | 2006 | Change |
|---|---|---|---|---|
| Total | 745 | 770 | 778 | +33 |
| African American | 707 | 722 | 740 | +33 |
| Asian | 825 | 862 | 888 | +63 |
| Filipino | 771 | 827 | 837 | +66 |
| Hispanic | 651 | 689 | 697 | +46 |
| White (not Hispanic) | 797 | 830 | 837 | +40 |

*2002 is the first year that the California Department of Education posted summative data for districts as a whole.

# CHAPTER THREE

# What's in It for Me?

*A nurturing school climate has the power to overcome incredible risk factors in the lives of children. What is far less acknowledged is that creating this climate for students necessitates creating this environment for all school personnel.*

—Benard, 1993, p. 48

I often talk with educators about rethinking schooling, using resilience as a lens.

Think about the compromises you make in your teaching every day. Compare this to what your hopes and dreams were when you first entered teaching. These compromises are not your fault! The dailyness of schooling, the large number of students, the focus on teaching the curriculum over meeting the needs of children, the way teaching is so isolated from other adults all make it very difficult to know students well enough not to have to compromise every day. It is important to remember, however, that it is also not the fault of the students, the parents, or the administrators. The system has to change.

Think about the kind of world you want to live in. We all want to live and work in places where people know us well, where expectations are high and support to meet those expectations are focused and purposeful, and where our voices are valued. Our students want the same conditions in their lives. The core of any school reform effort has to be based on creating these conditions for your students and for you.

Resilience is about building a community that is rich in the protective factors of caring, high expectations, purposeful support, and ongoing opportunities for participation. To accomplish this, it is important that we adults support our own resilience; we need these protective factors, too.

*What's in it for me,* whether I am a teacher, an administrator, a parent, a student, a grandparent, a school board member, a community member, is the opportunity to help build a community, with and for my neighbors and for myself, that is rich in the protective factors so that we all can have a more hopeful future. I am a teacher; I was an administrator; I am a parent; I like to think that I am always a student; I am a grandparent; I have sat on several boards; and I am a community member. I want to live in a place where people care about each other, where expectations and support are high, and where our participation is valued. I want this in my home, in my work place, and in the community where I live.

This must include taking care of myself. For the fourteen years I was a high school principal, I worked very hard to build a resilient community for students, staff, and parents; I did this before I knew what resilience theory was. At the same time, I never found time for lunch, I exercised irregularly, I found too little time for my wife, and I know I found little time for myself. What's in it for me is to continue receiving the good feelings that come with *giving*, but also to do some *receiving* as well. For educators to build a school culture that fosters resilience, we must create the conditions for ourselves as well as for students. For adults to be effective we too need to love well, work well, play well, and expect well.

If I am a professional educator working at a school rich in the protective factors of resilience, the following benefits will be at the core of the school culture.

## COLLEGIALITY

> *I think that the problem of how to change things from "I" to "we," of how to bring a good measure of collegiality and relatedness to adults who work in schools, is one that belongs on the national agenda of school improvement—at the top. It belongs at the top because the relationships amongst adults*

*in schools are the basis, the precondition, the* sine qua non
*that allow, energize, and sustain all other attempts at school
improvement. Unless adults talk with one another, observe
one another, and help one another, very little will change.*

—Barth, 1991, p. 32

Bring a group of educators into a room for a professional development activity, and you cannot shut them up. They do not want to listen to a presentation. They want to talk with each other! Why? Because teachers and administrators have very little time to engage other adults in meaningful conversation. Teachers and administrators have little

> What kind of support do you expect from people you work with? How well do you know the work of people you work with? How well do they know your work?

expectation and little time to share ideas, successes, or concerns with each other. Practice is very private.

An important part of building a resilient school community is to create the time and expectation for teachers and administrators as professionals to be with other teachers and administrators in order to know each other and their work well. True professionals share practice and generate much of their own knowledge base; engineers do this; doctors do this; lawyers do this.

Professional development should be based on teachers sharing their work and the work of their students. Teachers need to watch each other teach, serve as peer coaches, develop curriculum together, plan instruction together, assess student work together, and engage in collaborative action research. Teachers should work together to develop expectations for what every student needs to know and design multiple assessment strategies to help demonstrate when students are meeting school standards and to guide strategies for helping students who are not.

Parents, community members, students, and classified staff (an often left out, valuable member of the school community) also should to be involved with the school professionals, sharing concerns and expertise, also getting to know each other and their work well. This involves school professionals truly getting to know and understand the cultures that exist within the communities we serve.

## INTELLECTUAL STIMULATION

In a school rich in the protective factors, adults challenge each other to be reflective, to share ideas, to ask good questions, to read widely, to think deeply. Adults challenge each other to know each student and his or her work well and, just as important, to know each adult and his or her work well.

> What do you do to build professional relationships? Do you enjoy "talking shop"? Does such talk help make you more effective? Whom do you work with who challenges you to think about what you do?

If the primary purpose of schooling is, as Ted Sizer (1985) says, to learn to use your mind well, then it must start with the school professionals. Few of us have had school experience in using our minds well. Few of us have developed the habits of mind that I would put as the focus for student learning. Even with my Phi Beta Kappa key, as a student I was expected to do very little serious, rigorous work until graduate school. I became very proficient at memorizing and giving back to the teacher what had been lectured to me. How can we ask students to do that which we cannot? Deborah Meier (1995) offers the Meier mandate:

> No school shall have graduation requirements that cannot be met by every professional working in the school, and therefore these requirements shall be phased in only as fast as the school can bring its staff up to the standards it requires of its students. (p.183)

## VOICE

It is unlikely that any school will foster resilience unless the members of that school community have significant voice over the workings of that community. This is particularly true for teachers. Teachers currently have the traditional voice over their classrooms that comes with the

> Do you feel listened to at work? Who values your opinion? How do they show you? Do you value what others have to say? How do you let them know?

privacy of practice that results when a teacher shuts the classroom door. They should also have voice in the work of peers that comes from knowing colleagues and their work well. Teachers are professionals, and professionals should have collaborative say over their work lives. When teachers know that their voices are valued in the daily workings of the school, they are much more open to the voices of students, parents, classified staff, and community members.

## RESPECT

Most schools are not very respectful places.

- Teachers and classified staff do not feel respected by students, administrators, parents, or the community.
- Students do not feel respected by most adults in school and, for the most part, do not feel respected by the community or at times by their parents.
- Parents do not feel respected by school personnel and, too often, do not feel respected by their own children.
- Principals do not feel respected by most teachers, students, parents, and district office personnel.

In a resilient learning community, the culture of the school is built on respect. If teachers and administrators know each other and their work well, if students, classified staff, parents, and community members know that they are valued as participants in the school, if the conditions are in place to support students learning to use their minds and hearts well, if students and their work are known well, school personnel will feel recog-

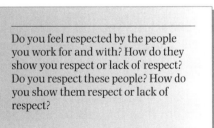

Do you feel respected by the people you work for and with? How do they show you respect or lack of respect? Do you respect these people? How do you show them respect or lack of respect?

nized as professionals, parents as collaborators, and students as the central focus of the school.

# INCREASED JOB SATISFACTION

When teachers and administrators work to know students and student work well, when they commit to help every student learn to use her or his mind and heart well, the conversation changes. You no longer hear blaming of parents and students. You no longer hear blaming of peers and administrators. As the protective factors of resilience become central to a school community for

> What and who bring you joy at work? What do you do to build these people and these activities into your daily work life?

the children and the adults, you can see, hear, feel, taste, and smell the difference in a school. You see teachers and administrators engaging peers, students, parents, classified staff, and community in the support of student learning. You hear decisions being made based on what is best for students, based on consideration of the needs of individual students. You feel the satisfaction that teachers sense when talking about how rewarding it is to work with their students because the students are growing and are appreciative, as are the parents, the principal, and the community. You can almost taste and smell the satisfaction when members of the school community repeat Maria's words, "They really trust me here."

# SHARED OWNERSHIP AND LEADERSHIP

As the benefits just described become more central to the culture of your school, you will feel increased ownership for the learning of all students and adults. You will want and be expected to share in the leadership of the school. This requires skills, attitudes, and behaviors that are new to many teachers and administrators. A detailed explanation is beyond the scope of this book. However, there are several excellent books on this topic. *Leadership Capacity for Lasting School Improvement* by Linda Lambert (2003) and *Awakening the Sleeping Giants* by Marilyn Katzenmeyer and Gayle Moller (2001) are excellent resources. My new book *Building Leadership Capacity: How Teachers Can Foster Equitable Schools* (Krovetz & Arriaza, 2006) focuses on teachers writing about their emergence as skilled teacher-leaders.

# OBSTACLES

In my opinion the key obstacles to creating resilient learning communities are

1. deeply held beliefs and practices that indicate that not all students are believed capable of using their minds and hearts well;

2. schools that are too large to support knowing each student well;

3. schools that are too large to support teachers, staff, administrators, and parents knowing each other well;

4. lack of time for professional educators to know each other and their work well;

5. lack of time for professional educators to know students well;

6. popular public belief that public schools are failing and that the solution is outside of the school—top-down solutions.

## Deeply Held Beliefs

If you use the following questions to assess your school, particularly if you insist on specific evidence, you will learn a lot about the belief system that guides the daily practices of the school.

- How successful is your school in meeting the needs of your students?
- Which students are you doing an excellent job for? Which students could you serve better?
- What specific evidence do you have to support your answers to these two questions?
- What is blocking your school from being more successful?
- What are the underlying beliefs of your school culture that support these blocks?
- What needs to change for your school to be more successful?
- What specific evidence do you have to support your answers to these last three questions?

All important school redesign efforts should begin with a serious study of the underlying beliefs of the staff, parents, and students. If we do not believe deep in our hearts that all students are capable of learning to use their minds and hearts well, meaningful school change will not occur and last. Often, change efforts start with a mission statement, arrived at by broad-based consensus. What I am proposing requires a much more in-depth look at one's beliefs and practices. One needs to be open to courageous conversations about institutional racism (Singleton, 2006). Without these very hard conversations, the deep underpinnings of the school culture will not change and the practices that block success for all students will not be addressed. Answering the questions just asked, particularly seeking a wide variety of evidence to back up your answers, will require honesty and usually a fundamental change in our expectations for students and ourselves. Collecting evidence is discussed in Chapter 7.

Many current school practices and circumstances indicate that we do not believe that all students are capable:

- Some of these school practices—ability grouping in particular—are sacred to many parents and to many teachers. Yet tracking students by ability sends a very clear message to students that rigorous study is available to and expected of only the select few. Tracking is discussed in more detail in Chapter 5.
- We are still in a world that too often discourages females, students of color, and English language learning students from taking certain "demanding" courses.
- A key impact of NCLB is that considerable time at many schools is spent preparing students for high-stakes, standardized tests. If we really value students using their minds and hearts well, we need to assess their ability to do so.
- A second impact of NCLB is that, particularly for students from high-risk environments, the curriculum has shrunk to include little other than reading and math. Science, history, and the arts have been severely reduced in the curriculum.
- A third impact of NCLB is that, particularly for teachers in schools serving students from high-risk environments, teachers are expected to strictly follow scripted curricula. The result is that the professionalism of teachers is greatly reduced.

Thus, truly looking at, questioning, and changing one's deeply held beliefs are the most difficult obstacles to overcome, because they reflect so clearly on what we expect from ourselves, as well as from our students.

## School Size

- What percentage of the students at your school does the principal know by name?
- What percentage of the students do most teachers know by name?
- What percentage of the teachers and classified staff do all teachers and classified staff know by name?

The school size issue is also heavily ingrained. Athletic, music, and advanced placement programs, all potentially very valuable for helping certain students learn to use their minds and hearts well, are based on having a large student population to select from. Yet, the success of small schools of choice throughout the United States, especially those serving students from high-risk environments, attest to the power of quality small schools (Cotton, 1996; Klonsky, 1996; Meier, 1995; Wasley & Lear, 2001). Debbie Meier writes, "Large schools neither nourish the spirit nor educate the mind. . .what big schools do is remind most of us that we don't count for a lot. . . . Small school size is not only a good idea but an absolute prerequisite for qualitative change in deep-seated habits" (p. 107).

The most important prerequisite for developing a resilient learning community is the underlying belief in each child's ability. The second most important prerequisite is to know each child and his or her work well. When both of these prerequisites are in place, every child can be viewed as the responsibility of every person at the school. If I could recommend only one structural change that I think is most crucial to improve the quality of learning for our students, especially those students in urban schools, it would be to rethink schools so that the maximum enrollment at any school would not exceed four hundred students.

Anzar is an example of a high-quality small school that is doing wonderful work. The case studies in Chapter 5 are about three other small schools that are doing wonderful work.

## Time

Time is without a doubt the most valuable resource for school improvement. Thoughtfulness is time-consuming; collaboration is time-consuming.

Look at how time is used at your school.

- How engaging are staff meetings at your school? Leadership team meetings? Home and school club meetings? Professional development activities?
- How much time do teachers spend working with individual students or students in small groups, really getting to know students and their work well?
- How much time do teachers spend working with other teachers in small groups, really getting to know teachers and their work well?

School leaders should remember that every time they gather people for a meeting, they are modeling teaching behavior. If school leaders choose to consistently run meetings from the front of the room, the message to teachers is that teacher-led, whole-group instruction is okay. If school leaders choose to consistently give information at meetings, the message to teachers is that information giving is okay as the primary teaching strategy. Good leaders model desired behaviors at every opportunity.

Resilient school communities set aside time for students and staff to know each other well. A strong student advisory program, summer common planning days, and quality use of meeting time, as exemplified by Anzar High School, allows teachers and students to work together on school issues and for an adult and a small number of students to get to know each other over several years. At a large senior or junior high school, with large class sizes and six-, seven-, or eight-period days, an advisory period may be seen as one more responsibility on top of the dailyness of dealing with 150-plus students per day. Many middle and high schools are changing the way they use school time, however, with the result being that teachers teach fewer students.

Many schools use professional development days and/or schedule a weekly time when students start school late or leave early for staff to work together. Too often these days are not focused, and teachers attend with minimal expectations. However, we have learned what "best practice" is for professional development (Speck & Knipe, 2005) and, in schools like those described in this book, where time is used to look at student work and at student needs and to get to know each other's work well, time used productively pays off in student learning.

## Popular Beliefs and Simple Solutions to Complex Problems

The popular, and perhaps true, perception that many public schools, particularly inner-city schools, are failing has led many people to question the role of public schools. Should schools only teach "basic academic skills," and if so which ones, or should a school try to protect students from many of the societal problems that they bring to the school? Is it the school's responsibility to teach driver's education, AIDS prevention, smoking cessation, conflict resolution, critical thinking, music, art, vocational skills. . . ? What should be on this list and who should decide are at the forefront of the educational agenda for most states and for our nation.

Many educators, myself included, believe very strongly that the top-down approach undermines school improvement efforts, has little positive, long-term impact on student learning, and will probably speed the movement to publicly financed charter schools. Long lists of what every student should know and tests that objectively measure this will not lead to schools knowing students well and challenging students to use their minds and hearts well. It will lead and has led to teaching to the test. When I was in ninth and tenth grade, living in New York State, I took New York Regents Exams. My world history teacher finished lecturing from the textbook in January, and we took practice exams for the second half of the course. I did very well on the Regents Exam, forgot a lot of facts the day after, and left the class with little appreciation for the importance of history.

Real improvement will come when a community agrees that every student is capable of using his or her mind and heart well, that the protective factors of resilience are needed by all students and adults, and commits to making this happen. Beware of simple fixes for complex problems! Creating resilient learning communities is not a simple fix!

## WHAT DOES IT LOOK LIKE?

The next three chapters describe what schools look like that are caring, have high expectations and purposeful support, and value participation. I cannot offer a simple list of three things that would make the school more caring and three for high expectations and three for participation. Building a resilient learning community is about deeply held beliefs, school culture, and daily practice. Much needs to change if schools are to truly foster resilience. The case studies at the end of each chapter in this book describe schools that I believe are centered on fostering resilience in students.

After reading the next three chapters, you should be able to answer the following questions:

- What would a school look like whose culture is centered on the principles of resilience?
- What would curriculum, instruction, and assessment be like in a school that is designed to foster resilience for all students?
- How would teacher and administrator roles change in such a school?

As you read the examples of what I look for in each of the next three chapters (They are listed as a whole in Resource A), you are encouraged to think of specific evidence that these exist at your school. You might want to think very personally about items and ask yourself, "How do I/we . . .?" and "Why do I/we . . .?"

## WHY ME?

We all make compromises in our lives that help us cope with the obstacles that confront us. We also decide what is worth fighting for. Whenever any of us compromises on our commitment to the youth of our community, the future for our youth becomes less hopeful. All youth—all people—need the protective factors of resilience in our lives. We need them in our family, community, and school. Let this serve as my sermon for the day.

Ted Sizer (1985, 1992, 1996) does an excellent job of describing the compromises made by Horace, a hypothetical, fine high school English teacher and the ways that Horace comes to grips with these compromises and works to uncompromise.

## WHAT DO I DO FIRST?

Chapter 7 deals with the issues of change. you can start with the following steps, however:

1. Self-assess

   Assess and challenge your own deeply held beliefs about whether you believe in your head and in your heart that all students are capable of using their minds and hearts well. Assess and question your deeply held beliefs about how you learn. Require that you collect real evidence to back up your initial thoughts on this.

2. Talk, talk, talk

   Hold what I call "essential conversations" with whomever will reflect with you. As you challenge your deeply held beliefs, ask hard questions of yourself and your friends. Ask hard questions within your family, community, and school. Use the prompts in this book. Require evidence when people make definitive statements. The more you talk, and particularly listen, the clearer your own belief system will become.

3. Read, read, read

   The bibliography at the end of this book offers numerous suggestions for books and articles you can read that will challenge your belief system. Pass the readings on.

4. Talk some more

   Keep the essential conversations alive.

5. Prepare to lead

   Do not allow the typical compromises that educators, students, parents, and the community make because of lack of will to occur within your family, community, and schools.

# WILL THERE BE PUBLIC SCHOOLS IN THE TWENTY-FIRST CENTURY?

I have heard that six out of ten parents would send kids to private schools if they had the money to do so. Even though voucher initiatives have failed at the polls in several states, the concept of public funding for private schooling is still commonly heard in the media and in election campaigns. Charter schools are opening in many communities, blurring the distinction between public and private schools. Yet quality public schooling is at the heart of a democracy. Every child, regardless of wealth, race, ethnicity, sex, religion, handicap, sexual preference, or primary language deserves the opportunity to learn to use his or her mind and heart well.

Public schools will be preserved as a cornerstone of U.S. democracy if citizens like us assess, question, and adjust our deeply held beliefs about the purpose of schooling, and work to build resilient learning communities that we come to know well. Ownership creates responsibility, commitment, and hopefulness.

# CASE STUDY: TWO OAK GROVE SCHOOLS

In the last chapter you read about the commitment of the Oak Grove School District educational community to close the achievement gap. In this chapter you will read about two Oak Grove Schools. I asked Ginny Maiwald, director of special education and former Edenvale principal, to describe the Adopt-A-College program that has existed at Edenvale since 1991. A more thorough case study of Edenvale School can be found in Topf, Maiwald, and Krovetz (2004). I also asked Robert Topf, principal of Parkview School and also a former Edenvale principal, to write about how Parkview is closing the achievement gap. When reading these case studies, you will hopefully understand the power of a cohesive district effort to improve the learning of all students and how two schools have done this in ways that foster resilience for students and adults.

## Edenvale School

At Edenvale Elementary School, academic, behavioral, and professional expectations are high. You feel this when you speak to the teachers and administration. For over fifteen years, the school has provided the message that even if your parents have not gone to college, regardless of family background, you can graduate high school and attend college or a postsecondary vocational program.

*Through the Eyes of the Student*

Juwan races to school. He must get in the breakfast line early so that he is ready for the school year's first Adopt-A-College Program Assembly. Juwan's mind is racing. He must remember his lines perfectly. This morning his class asks the principal's permission to participate in the Adopt-A-College Program. His class has written a rap about going to college. This is one of his favorite days of the school year. He will get to meet his college pen pal, as well as, important former Edenvale students. Juwan watches his teacher become emotional and tearful as the former Edenvale students greet their teachers and pay tribute to this school and program that has provided the educational foundation for their current success. They are present to tell their college stories and the importance of working hard during the elementary school years.

The former students remind Juwan about the importance of doing his personal best, an important behavioral guideline at the school. Some of the former students have traveled far to join in this college day event. One former student, Christopher, is wearing his U.S. military uniform. Juwan sits in awe of the image that Chris's presence creates in the school cafeteria. His uniform is immaculate. As Chris passes by, Juwan notices his shoes. Chris has the shiniest shoes Juwan has ever seen. Juwan cannot pull his eyes from the image of Chris saluting the American flag. Juwan wonders what it would feel like to wear such a uniform and walk in those shoes.

As the San Jose State football team strides past Juwan's class, an African American player stops and gives Juwan a high five. On this day, everyone at Edenvale wears a college shirt provided by donations from colleges across the country. Later, Juwan is selected to help lead the San Jose State University (SJSU) cheer. This is the university Juwan's pen pal attends. Juwan has been to SJSU for a special tour. Juwan has also seen pictures of SJSU on TV, and his pen pal has written to answer all his questions about the campus.

The assembly begins and his class takes the stage. The audience begins clapping along with the rap and follows the words.

The energy in the cafeteria grows, and soon everyone is absorbed in the power of this day. Juwan stands at the front of the stage and delivers his lines. Everyone applauds. Next, Bobby Sanders, the state's 126-pound power weightlifting champion takes the stage, performing to music and delivering his message about a healthy lifestyle and drug-free body. Like Juwan, Bobby is African American.

*Throught the Eyes of School Leadership*

Former students have given speeches, and each class has performed. One class performed a rap, another, a PowerPoint presentation, and a third, a skit. Each class expressed its desire to participate in the Adopt-A-College Program. The former principal concludes the program with a heartfelt song performed on guitar and sung uniquely for the Edenvale students, staff, and parents.

*Through the Eyes of the Family*

Everyone joins in the song to the tune of "Johnny B. Goode." It speaks of hard work and perseverance. Juwan replaces the name Johnny with his own name and hums the tune throughout the day and into the evening. The family's small apartment echoes with Juwan's version of the new Edenvale song. His little sister imitates his singing and Juwan speaks to her about going to college. Juwan has absorbed the message about college and convinced his family about his plan. As Juwan reluctantly takes off his college T-shirt at the end of the day, he knows in his heart that he wants a college education to be a part of his future.

These elementary school students write to college buddies, participate in special assemblies, and visit college campuses. They are beginning to integrate a personal expectation that college is a part of their future. When this program began fifteen years ago, 27 percent of the students from this school went on to college. This fall, 85 percent of Edenvale students were accepted to colleges and universities throughout the nation. This school culture emanates a heartfelt theme that our students will be successful learners.

**Edenvale School**
285 Azucar Ave.
San Jose, CA 95111
408-227-7060
Web site: www.ogsd.k12.ca.us

| **Enrollment:** | | **607** | | |
|---|---|---|---|---|
| Asian | | 10% | | |
| Hispanic | | 74% | | |
| White (not Hispanic) | | 6% | | |

| *API* | *1999* | *2005* | *2006* | *Change* |
|---|---|---|---|---|
| Total | 604 | 720 | 755 | +151 |
| Hispanic | 510 | 697 | 731 | +221 |
| White (not Hispanic) | NA | NA | NA | NA |
| Asian | NA | NA | NA | NA |

## Eliminating the Achievement Gap at Park Elementary School

Welcome to Parkview Elementary, home of the **PANTHERS**. The PANTHER motto developed by our students is **P**repared, **A**wesome, **N**ever give up, **T**alented, **H**ere every day, **E**xcellent, **R**esponsible, and **S**mart. It reflects the high expectations that we have for students, staff, and families. The 700 students are a model of cultural diversity. Fall 2006 demographics were 36 percent Hispanic, 32 percent Asian, 17 percent white, 6 percent Filipino, 7 percent African American, 1 percent Pacific Islander, and 6 percent multiple/no response. Thirty-six percent of our students qualify for free or reduced lunches. We have over 250 English learners, 70 gifted and talented, and 35 special education students. Students, staff, and community share a vision of a "safe, academically focused community of learners who deeply appreciate diverse cultures. We feature engaging instruction, producing skilled readers and writers, and powerful mathematicians, with the knowledge, talent, and problem-solving skills for academic excellence and for making a positive impact in the world."

For several years, we have had an overarching district theme: eliminate the achievement gap between Latino and African heritage students and the students from white and Asian backgrounds. Our approach to this has been to increase the performance of all students, while accelerating the learning of the underachieving students of Latino and African heritage. What follows is a description of the efforts at Parkview (see Figure 3.1).

*Focus on Race and Equity*

Courageous conversations about race and equity have been a major thrust of professional development at both district- and school-site levels. Staff is encouraged to explore their own racial identities, engage in the emotionally charged dialogue about white privilege, and reflect upon racist and antiracist educational structures and practices. This is of particular importance as a primarily white instructional staff is teaching a student population composed of 83 percent students of color. This type of adult learning focusing on educator belief systems and principles of equity is an ongoing process.

An essential tenet to eliminating the achievement gap is for the teaching staff to truly believe that all students can achieve the high standards that we have established for them. For the last three years, teachers have been involved in cycle of inquiry work. Each teacher selects three Latino or African heritage focal students achieving at the basic level. He or she organizes instruction and evaluates the success of his or her lessons with those three students in mind. Teachers meet in teams to analyze the results of interim assessments, view student work, and select focal standards and strategies to move those students toward proficiency. Considerable emphasis has been placed on developing cultural competency, with staff seeking to understand our students and families in light of their unique racial and cultural backgrounds. By developing multiple perspectives and establishing a classroom and school environment where Latino and African heritage students see themselves reflected in the curriculum, on the walls, and throughout the school, these groups feel more highly valued.

**Figure 3.1**     Equity, Instruction, and Culturally Responsive Teaching to Close the Achievment Gap Focus: "Increase the learning of all students while accelerating the learning of students of Latino and African heritage"

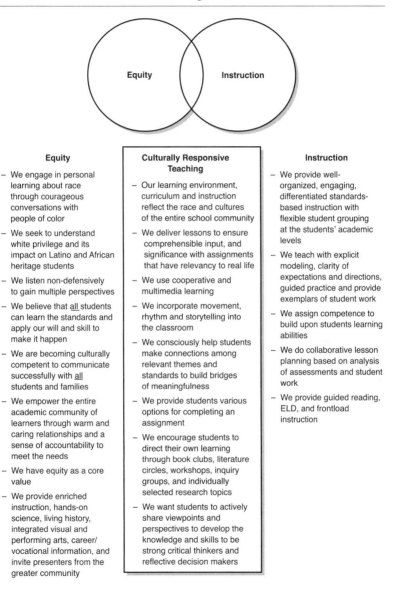

**Equity**

– We engage in personal learning about race through courageous conversations with people of color

– We seek to understand white privilege and its impact on Latino and African heritage students

– We listen non-defensively to gain multiple perspectives

– We believe that all students can learn the standards and apply our will and skill to make it happen

– We are becoming culturally competent to communicate successfully with all students and families

– We empower the entire academic community of learners through warm and caring relationships and a sense of accountability to meet the needs

– We have equity as a core value

– We provide enriched instruction, hands-on science, living history, integrated visual and performing arts, career/vocational information, and invite presenters from the greater community

**Culturally Responsive Teaching**

– Our learning environment, curriculum and instruction reflect the race and cultures of the entire school community

– We deliver lessons to ensure comprehensible input, and significance with assignments that have relevancy to real life

– We use cooperative and multimedia learning

– We incorporate movement, rhythm and storytelling into the classroom

– We consciously help students make connections among relevant themes and standards to build bridges of meaningfulness

– We provide students various options for completing an assignment

– We encourage students to direct their own learning through book clubs, literature circles, workshops, inquiry groups, and individually selected research topics

– We want students to actively share viewpoints and perspectives to develop the knowledge and skills to be strong critical thinkers and reflective decision makers

**Instruction**

– We provide well-organized, engaging, differentiated standards-based instruction with flexible student grouping at the students' academic levels

– We teach with explicit modeling, clarity of expectations and directions, guided practice and provide exemplars of student work

– We assign competence to build upon students learning abilities

– We do collaborative lesson planning based on analysis of assessments and student work

– We provide guided reading, ELD, and frontload instruction

*Powerful Instruction*

A strong tradition of teachers providing a thoughtful, well-organized, standards-based instructional program is in place at our school. The teaching staff has remained relatively stable through the years. Teachers value maximum time on task and make the learning come alive. Research-based instructional practices and strategies such as differentiated instruction and flexible grouping, guided reading, writing workshop, frontloading for English learners, extended literacy and mathematics instructional periods, a tightly organized home reading incentive program, living history, and multiple hands-on classroom activities inspire Parkview students to have a passion for learning. Parkview teachers recognize individual differences in learning styles, and constantly seek ways to help students' master standards. These practices have been vital to our work in closing the achievement gap. Before-school literacy academies taught by Parkview's resource specialist and collaboration between specialists and classroom teachers have provided effective safety nets, assisting students in reaching proficiency in academic standards.

*Enrichment*

A variety of enrichment activities are in place to help make the learning come alive and reach all students. The teaching staff and community value learning activities that enrich the general academic program and develop the talents of our students. For the last seven years, families have raised funds to support a three-day-a-week vocal and music history teacher. Each classroom is visited by a scientist from the community who delivers highly engaging hands-on science experiments aligned with grade-level science standards. For the past two years, teachers have run a lunchtime African American History Club. There are multiple after school recreation, sports, visual and performing arts clubs such as Families United in Dancing, The Knitting Club, Panther Basketball Teams, and the Music Bus offering piano and guitar classes. Parkview is also proud to have the only afterschool Vietnamese Heritage Language Program teaching Vietnamese literacy to eighty students, and a Spanish-language class as an additional enrichment.

*Community Involvement*

To say that Parkview parents and the community at large are actively involved in the school is indeed an understatement. The principal and staff recognize the importance of staying closely connected with the community and the need for outside energy to sustain momentum toward our mission of each student achieving his or her potential. Six active parent organizations contribute immensely to the overall success of the school. Along with the School Site Council, the Parkview School Community Association serves as an umbrella organization to four smaller cultural parent groups. The principal and members of the teaching staff meet on a regular basis in a Koffee Klatch of African heritage families, with the Las Culturas Spanish-speaking parent group, Parkview Vietnamese Community Association, and SANGAM, a Southeast Asian parent group. These groups reach out to families to ensure that race, language, and cultural differences do not impede the meaningful involvement of families in their children's academic success. Each of the cultural groups has representation in the Parkview School Community Association. Parents raise funds of approximately $45,000 per year to provide much of the enrichment at the school. Parents serve as academic mentors to students, write grants to support technology, and help with duplication and other clerical tasks. Community groups enhance the educational experience for Parkview students with programs such as conflict-resolution workshops, art, information about the water supply, public transportation, park rangers, and college nights.

*Caring Learning Environment*

Parkview students are expected to be safe and caring and to always demonstrate their personal best in their learning and behavior. An important theme at the school is honoring and celebrating everyone's cultural heritage. Students are encouraged to feel proud of their unique racial and ethnic backgrounds and family traditions and to appreciate and learn about the backgrounds of their classmates. Parkview teachers build strong relationships with students. Buddy classes are established where older students assist in the learning of younger students.

Through this brief description of Parkview, you capture a glimpse of how we are striving to eliminate the achievement gap. Through consistent effort, professionalism, and success, staff seems to have developed a sense of collective efficacy. In other words, when we put our minds and hearts behind reaching a goal, we can achieve that goal. If you walk through and explore the school, you will see talented teachers providing stimulating curricula, aligned in every subject area with state content standards. You will recognize well-organized instruction within and across grade levels, experience highly engaged students discussing each other's writing, observe students solving challenging real life math problems, and be impressed by how hard our students are working to reach proficient to advanced levels of achievement. You will see meaningful parent involvement as you watch the academic mentors nurturing our students' reading development. You will experience a powerful community of learners dedicated to the mission of each student reaching his or her maximum learning potential.

## Parkview School
330 Bluefield Drive
San Jose, CA 95136
408-226-4655
Web site: www.ogsd.k12.ca.us

| **Enrollment**: | **700** |
|---|---|
| Hispanic | 36% |
| Asian | 32% |
| White | 17% |
| African American | 7% |
| Filipino | 6% |
| Pacific Islander | 1% |

| API | 1999 | 2005 | 2006 | Change |
|---|---|---|---|---|
| Total | 760 | 807 | 831 | +71 |
| Hispanic | 597 | 707 | 740 | +143 |
| White (not Hispanic) | 805 | 864 | 852 | +47 |
| Asian | 828 | 856 | 891 | +63 |

CHAPTER FOUR

# I Care, You Care, We All Care— But How Do Students Know?

*This place hurts my spirit.*

—Poplin & Weeres, 1994, p. 11

*Human relationships are the heart of schooling. The inter-*
*actions that take place between students and teachers and*
*among students are more central to student success than*
*any method of teaching literacy, or science, or math. When*
*powerful relationships are established between teachers and*
*students, these relationships frequently can transcend the*
*economic and social disadvantages that afflict communities*
*and schools alike in inner city and rural areas.*

—Cummins, 1996, p. 1

Throughout my schooling, I was motivated primarily by grades. If a teacher had told me to stick my head through a glass window to earn an A, I would have looked questioningly at the teacher and then run to the head of the line to do so. Most students are not motivated by grades, however. Most students are motivated to work in school by the relationships they establish with teachers and peers. One of the important lessons I learned as a high school teacher and principal is that the majority of students work hard for teachers they like and respect and from whom they feel respect, and they do not work hard for teachers when the student does not feel respected—and students decide very quickly if a teacher is worth working for. Thus, the heart of teaching is really about establishing bonds and relationships with students. Norm Lezin, the former CEO of Salz Tannery in Santa Cruz, California, says that a good school is one at which "adults are wrapped around students" because "only relationships change people."

Teachers do make a difference in the lives of students, and, as Judith Deiro (2005) reminds us, our influence is based on the connections we make with them. A close bond with a competent, emotionally stable caregiver is essential in the lives of children who overcome great adversity. Emmy Werner found that after a family member, a favorite teacher was reported to be the most positive role model. Thus, it is important that teachers look for the strengths and possibilities within each child and that means at times to look beyond the hostility in some youth to the insecurities that lie underneath. I was struck by comments made by Steve Wozniak, cofounder of Apple Computer Company, regarding three heroes in his life. He listed his fourth- and fifth-grade teacher, a high school electronics teacher, and his father. The secret, once again, is to know the student well.

The words of Mervlyn Kitashima, one of Werner and Smith's resilient children, are presented in Figure 4.1.

In this chapter and in the next two chapters, I present brief lists of the kinds of things I look for when I visit a school. I asked friends and colleagues to help me develop these lists. The lists are presented together as observational tools in Resource A. No item on these lists is sacred. The one sacred premise is the belief in the potential of all students to learn to use their minds and hearts well.

**Figure 4.1**   Excerpts from "The Faces of Resiliency" by Mervlyn Kitashima (1997), one of the participants in Emmy Werner and Ruth Smith's study.

My Grandma Kahaunaele is the only person I remember who would comb my hair. I remember going to school one day and the teacher said to me, "Doesn't anybody ever comb your hair? Doesn't anybody ever wash your face?" I guess I was dirty. Grandma Kahaunaele was the only one who would comb my hair. You know, Hawaiian girls always have long hair, and I had long hair, but it was always tangled, and it was always dirty. I remember sitting in the playground, first grade, and wondering why my head was so itchy. It's because it was so dirty. Back then I'd scratch and scratch. Grandma Kahaunaele was the one who would wash my hair, and she was the only one who would take the tangles out. She would sit me down at her knee and she'd have this giant, yellow comb. She'd patiently take every tangle out of my hair. And for any of you who've had long, tangled hair, with a comb going through it, not fun, you know? Your head is yanking as it gets caught, and I'd be crying. She would say, "Almost pau, almost pau." Pau means finished. "Almost done." She would eventually get finished, and I remember feeling clean, and I remember feeling pretty, and I remember feeling like maybe somebody cares for me, even for just a little while.

Mervlyn was married at age sixteen and had her first child at age seventeen. Pregnant girls were not allowed to continue at school. The dean of students went to the counselor and insisted that the counselor begin the parent-student program that they had been discussing and that Mervlyn be the first student enrolled. Incidentally, Mervlyn has been married to the same person for twenty-six years. Her husband is a school teacher.

Mervlyn Kitashima is a district coordinator for the Parent-Community Networking Centers in Hawaii's Department of Education.

# WHAT WOULD A SCHOOL LOOK LIKE WHOSE CULTURE IS CENTERED ON CARING?

Henderson and Milstein (1996) list five categories of caring under the profile of a resilience-building school:

- Members have a sense of belonging.
- Cooperation is promoted.
- Celebration of successes are practiced.
- Leaders spend lots of positive time with members.
- Resources are obtained with a minimum of effort.

Whereas, I do believe that every school must set its own path toward fostering resilience and that there is no formula for making this happen, I also believe that certain beliefs and practices are characteristic of schools making a sincere effort to be caring communities. These practices are clearly reflected in daily practice and in school culture; they are not something people do for five minutes a day to display caring. When I wrote the first draft of this chapter, I began to write long lists under each category. I realized that I was practicing what I preach against. I was writing the *standards*. Therefore, I have chosen to list only four or five items in each category. These are things I look for when I visit a school.

> Shadow a student for a school day. Sit in classes, eat meals with the student, check out the restrooms, observe the peer relationships as a student does. What is it like to be a student at this school?

## All Have a Sense of Belonging

- Students talk freely about feeling respected, supported, and known by teachers, administrators, and peers.
- Teachers and classified staff talk easily about feeling respected, valued, supported, and known by administrators, peers, students, and parents. (Ask the custodian.)
- Teachers and classified staff feel included in discussions and decision making.
- Office staff is friendly and courteous to students, staff, parents, community, and visitors.

- Body language in the halls and in classrooms is unanxious—students are not afraid of other students; student body language does not change when adults approach.

## Cooperation Is Promoted

- Cross-age tutoring programs are in place to support student learning.
- Cooperative learning is taught and practiced in classes.
- Conflict resolution skills are taught and practiced throughout the school.
- Students are seen mixing easily across race, ethnicity, and gender.

## Celebration of Successes Is Practiced

- Lots of students, teachers, staff, parents, and community members are recognized for their contributions in a wide variety of ways.
- People use the word "we" when talking about the school.
- Positive communications go home from teachers and administrators regularly.
- People talk openly about what didn't work and what was learned.

## Leaders Spend Lots of Positive Time With Members

- Administrators are seen interacting with students in positive ways.
- Administrators know and use the names of all or most students.
- Teachers, students, parents, and staff talk about the principal seeming to be everywhere.
- Class continues when administrators walk in.

## Resources Are Obtained With a Minimum of Effort

- The campus is clean and orderly.
- There are lots of books in classrooms.

- Teachers report that the office staff is supportive of their teaching.
- The supply closet is open and copy machines are readily available.
- The library and computers are accessible to students, teachers, staff, and parents before and after school and during recess.

Linda Silvius, School Partnership Coordinator for Project Cornerstone (www. projectcornerstone.com) and Sara Truebridge, a doctoral student at Mills College in Oakland, California, suggest an exercise for considering the degree of caring at your school. Post a list of all student names. Give all staff—teachers, counselors, classified, administrators—colored dots. Ask

> Rate your own school or schools you know well using the checklist. Which are strengths for your school and what are the areas of concern?

them to place dots next to the names of students whom they know well and whom they think knows they care about them. Look at which names have dots by them and which do not, which have multiple dots, and which have few or none. This will tell you a lot about the breadth and depth of caring at your school.

## WHAT WOULD CURRICULUM, INSTRUCTION, AND ASSESSMENT BE LIKE IN A SCHOOL THAT IS CENTERED ON CARING?

Some people might argue that "caring" and "respect" are not the business of schools, that we need to focus on high academic standards to which all students are held accountable so that students will be prepared for the workforce of the twenty-first century. My response to this is threefold:

1. Being caring and respectful means guaranteeing as much as we can that every child can read, write, and compute;

2. Being caring and respectful means holding high expectations for every child regardless of race, ethnicity, gender, economic status, sexual preference, or learning disability;

3. If we want children to be caring and respectful, then we must provide schools that model caring and respect.

Debbie Meier (1995) argues,

> Caring and compassion are not soft, mushy goals. They are part of the hard core of subjects we are responsible for teaching. Informed and skillful care is learned. Caring is as much cognitive as affective. The capacity to see the world as others might is central to unsentimental compassion and at the root of both intellectual skepticism and empathy. . . . There is no tolerance without respect—and no respect without knowledge. (p. 63)

Nel Noddings (1995) makes a strong case that schools should organize around themes of caring rather than around the traditional disciplines.

What does it look like? Again, I kept my list short to reflect the key things I look for when I visit schools.

## Curriculum

- The work is meaningful to the students; students can tell you what they are doing and why; when asked, students will say that what they are learning is meaningful and meets their current and future life needs.
- Curriculum is integrated and thematic and focuses on a limited number of important content standards.
- Curriculum respects and acknowledges the ethnography and community of the students, using this as a departure point for curriculum that explores diversity of culture and opinion within and without the community.
- Students have choices in what they learn (curriculum), how they learn (instruction), and how they present what they have learned (assessment).

## Instruction

- Students are working, and teachers are coaching; that is students are actively engaged in work. I like the thought that students should work at least as hard as their teachers.

- Teachers move around the room and talk with individual students or with small groups of students.
- Students spend extended periods with the same teacher and with the same students.
- Time is provided for teachers to work together on developing instructional strategies, including peer coaching.

## Assessment

- Student work is displayed throughout the school.
- Students know and can articulate expectations teachers have for student learning. Most often rubrics are assessable and have been developed with student input.
- Students can be seen presenting what they have learned to others.
- Students have opportunities to demonstrate what they learn in meaningful ways, including self-reflection and participation in their own performance review.

> Rate your own school or schools you know well using the checklist. Which are strengths for your school and what are the areas of concern?

# WHAT DO TEACHER AND ADMINISTRATOR ROLES LOOK LIKE IN A SCHOOL FOCUSED ON CARING?

1. Decision making
   - Important decisions are made in a collaborative manner, involving all stakeholders in the decisions; one seldom hears, "We can't," "We aren't allowed," "I wasn't told." "I was told I have to . . ." "It's his or her fault."
   - Meetings designed to make decisions set aside adequate time for reflection, discussion, consensus building, and planning for action.
   - Ground rules for decision making are agreed upon, known, followed, and regularly reassessed.

- Conflict resolution strategies have been agreed upon, are taught, and are practiced.

2. Student discipline
   - Expectations for student behavior are reasonable, positive, public, known and enforced with consistency.
   - Classroom discipline is dealt with primarily by the classroom teacher; there are very few referrals to the office for disrespect.
   - The school "disciplinarian" does not spend the majority of his or her time disciplining students; rather he or she spends considerable time working positively with teachers, students, parents, and members of the community.
   - Student discipline is done privately, in a problem-solving mode.

3. Teacher as advisor
   - A strong student advisory system is in place. Advisories will not work in schools where teachers are responsible for large numbers of students.
   - Teachers maintain regular contact with parents regarding student progress, including positive feedback.
   - Teachers maintain regular contact with their students' other teachers. The school is organized in ways to support this communication.
   - Teachers, parents, and students collaborate to develop an individual learning plan for each student.

4. Teacher as collaborator
   - Teachers can be seen working in a collegial school culture—adults talk with one another, observe one another, help one another, laugh together, and celebrate together.
   - Conversations in the faulty room are lively, with teachers talking positively about students, student work, their own work, and the work of colleagues.
   - Faculty and staff are not seen brooding in the faculty room or in the parking lot or segregated by sex, race, department, or age.

- Time and resources are provided for teachers to collaborate.
- People talk openly about what didn't work and what was learned.

As stated in Chapter 1, resilient children usually have four attributes in common: social competence, problem-solving skills, autonomy, and a sense of purpose and future. A school that strives to be a resilient learning community builds its culture, designs curriculum, instruction, and assessment, and assigns roles and responsibilities that foster these four attributes. It is only when students and staff are known well and their work is known well that schools can truly do this.

> Rate your own school or schools you know well using the checklist. Which are strengths for your school and what are the areas of concern?

Resilient children are very good at seeking out and recruiting substitute parents. Teachers and school administrators need to be prepared to welcome these relationships. Schools should be places in which students and adults delight in each other's company. Resilient learning communities are such places.

## CASE STUDY: ROSEMARY SCHOOL AND CEZAR CHAVEZ SCHOOL

> *"Please tell how No Child Left Behind is making it harder to stay focused on doing what is best for our students."*

> —Rosemary teacher

The case studies presented here are about two urban elementary schools serving English language learning students. Both are located in communities identified by the high-risk environments students live in. Students in both schools are making large gains in achievement. Due to the criteria under NCLB both are identified as Program Improvement schools.

I began visiting Rosemary School before I began writing the first edition of this book. After several educational leaders in the

Campbell Elementary School District read Bonnie Benard's 1991 article, they told me that Rosemary is a resilient learning community and has been for thirty years. This seemed an exaggerated claim, given how difficult it is to maintain a positive school culture over time, particularly when the school clientele has largely changed in recent years as it had at Rosemary. The first case study at the end of this chapter is about Rosemary School. I began visiting Cesar Chavez School in Alum Rock School District in 1996 when I was asked to work with their staff on peer coaching around best literacy practices and with the school leadership team to help build a more positive school culture. This occurred as I was beginning my work on the first edition of this book.

In the first edition, Rosemary School was the case study at the end of Chapter 2 and Chavez at the end of Chapter 3. Because of the way NCLB is impacting both schools, and because of the similarities in their student populations, I decided to put both case studies in this chapter. The original case study for Rosemary is still in this chapter. The original case study for Chavez is in Resource F. What should stand out is how much the teachers at both schools care about their students.

## Rosemary School Written Spring 1998
## An Essential Conversation

What follows are parts of a conversation I had with Harriet Siegel, a retired teacher who taught at Rosemary School for twenty-two years (1966 to 1988) and was the school's reading specialist for most of that time. We were meeting for the first time and were sitting in a coffee shop in Campbell. I told her about my book, about how I had heard wonderful things about Rosemary School, and had visited a few times. I turned on my tape recorder and asked her to talk with me about why Rosemary is such a special school. The conversation, mostly Harriet talking to me, lasted for about an hour. *The comments in italics are my questions.* Pay special attention to her comments that relate to caring, high expectations and purposeful support, and valuing participation.

We looked for teachers who really cared about kids and knew curriculum second. That was our really big thing. The kids came first, and we tried to match the curriculum to the children, not the children to the curriculum.

Our school was in transition. The community was becoming very transient. One September there were seventy-five new kids coming in, and I met with the teachers. We decided to try four different approaches to reading. Each classroom was set up with appropriate materials. Each kid was tested and placed in a classroom that seemed appropriate for his mode of learning. It was a lot of work. The teachers had an openness to change. They were concerned about kids, and they were concerned about trying new things, and it worked!

I remember when the first Vietnamese students moved into Rosemary. We called parents and said we needed help. They brought us a professor of communication from the University of Saigon. We hired him as an aide. He is now head of bilingual education in a neighboring district. There were a variety of types of classrooms. We placed children where they would be comfortable. Teachers were very, very open. A kid might be in first grade for reading, third grade for math, own grade for social studies. We placed kids where their needs would be met. We were the first school in the state to have a program for Vietnamese students.

Being out of the classroom as a Miller Unruh teacher, I became involved in many professional activities. I became aware of all these nationally known people coming into the area. And what I did, I offered them $100 to come to Rosemary. And the teachers were very open to trying new things.

We were the only school, we were way ahead of the district, they never heard of staff development. They didn't know what it was. There was a core of teachers across grades. We worked together a lot. The principal was new, in his first principalship. He said he knew nothing about reading and turned the reading program over to me and to the teachers.

We fought with the district over retention. We wanted kids not judged by a policy. We always fought for an individual basis. That whole framework of what's best for the kid permeated everything.

Teachers were never punitive. They were always open to looking at why the kids did what they did.

We always took turkeys out to families at Thanksgiving time; teachers still do that. So much caring there.

*Where did this tremendous caring come from?*

From George, my first principal at Rosemary, and from Monroe, the psychologist. But we didn't have a lot of good principals.

Caring, the inservice, and the willingness of the teachers to try new things. Nothing was imposed on us. When we would see something new, we would talk about it. We would say: What do you think? Should we try it? What kind of materials do we need? That openness to trying new things benefited the kids. Teaching was never dull.

*The teachers had to feel safe in this school and district.*

Teachers were not afraid. It was really New York chutzpah.

We brought in good staff. No deadheads. You worked your head off, Saturdays and Sundays.

*Only a few teachers are left from the old days?*

Only three, one of whom is retiring this June.

*Yet the school is continuing on with deep caring about kids. Who has been passing this down from teacher to teacher?*

I know what we used to say. When people came to Rosemary, they became absorbed in the Rosemary culture. When teachers come, they don't do their thing, they do Rosemary's thing.

*So, as each group has come along. . . . Do you know how unusual that is? This has been going on for thirty years.*

Well, you know it was a joy teaching at Rosemary. It was a joyful experience.

*Because?*

Because of the kids. The kids loved coming to Rosemary, but they really came away with something. I remember feeling that people were crazy if they sent kids out to be happy and unable to read. I think the others felt the same. If you are allowed to be part of a supportive group, the creativity juices just flow. And if your focus is on kids, you just have it.

*How much do you think this has to do with Rosemary being the most diverse of Campbell's schools, and teachers feeling they are at Rosemary by choice?*

I think that this is an important part of it. There is a feeling of being needed and rewarded. Everything was hug time. I never enjoyed teaching anywhere as much as at Rosemary.

## Background Information (1998)

Rosemary School is the most culturally diverse of the eight elementary schools within the Campbell Elementary School District. The school consists of 530 students—49 percent Hispanic, 27 percent white, not Hispanic, 12 percent Asian, 11 percent African-American, 1 percent other. Ninety-five percent of the students receive free or reduced price lunches. Fifty-nine percent of the students are English language learners, speaking twenty-one different languages. Many years ago the school was primarily white, but lower-middle-class as compared to the middle-class students in the rest of the district. Later, the population shifted, and the school became predominantly Asian, Vietnamese in particular. In recent years, the population has shifted again and is primarily Hispanic.

During the 1996–1997 school year, Rosemary was totally rebuilt on the same piece of land that has housed Rosemary since 1952. The new $9.5 million building was designed to a great extent by the faculty and classified staff. "Art in Architecture" was a major emphasis during the construction. The banners in the lobby, the fence panels, the upstairs screens feature Rosemary children at play. The mobiles in the new exploratorium were created by Rosemary students, then enlarged and sculpted by Campbell Middle School students. State-of-the-art technology is part of every classroom.

Rosemary School has been identified as a Leadership School in literacy by the Noyce Foundation, is a California Distinguished School, received a state grant for school restructuring (SB 1274), and has a Title VII grant for bilingual and dual immersion education.

## Uniqueness of the School

*First Things First: The Head*

It should be clear from Harriet's words that the staff at Rosemary School believes deeply in the potential of each student. My observations have only confirmed that this belief is at the core of what each staff member brings to Rosemary daily. One day, I was talking with seven teachers about Rosemary. I said that I never heard negative talk about students. One teacher responded, "Negative talk is not *the Rosemary way.*" A second teacher said, "We would laugh a teacher out of the school for talking negatively about students." The other teachers laughed and agreed.

When I walk through classrooms, I observe all of the characteristics listed earlier in this chapter that demonstrate a belief in students' abilities to use their minds and hearts well. Student writing is hanging on walls and from the ceilings in classrooms; teachers are using appropriate questioning strategies; running records and other appropriate assessment strategies are being used to guide practice; interactive writing centers, writers workshops, literacy circles, and other excellent literacy strategies are evident in every classroom; students are active learners; students are working in cooperative groups; peer and cross-age tutoring is occurring.

Hiring the right people is critical. As Harriet stated, teachers new to Rosemary are expected to really care about kids and to work long hours. Given the implications of class size reduction in Grades K–3 and retirements, there has been a large turnover of staff. In 1997 of the twenty-three teachers, eight were in their first or second year. District and school support for beginning teachers is strong. Experience demonstrates that in most cases the hiring has been a good match, and, when it is not, the new teacher leaves for another school within the first two years.

*The Right Leg: Collegiality*

Unlike most schools, the faculty room is a delightful place to hang out. I hear and see the positive interactions among staff—the easy laughter, the positive conversations about kids, the sharing of ideas. This is more than the congeniality of peers who like each other, which they do; it is the collegiality of professionals who respect each other and support each other to do what is best for their students.

I have talked with most of the teachers. They feel that they have truly chosen education as their career. Several started in other careers (law, business) and switched to teaching. The principal talked with me about the ability of the teachers "to see what's in it for kids and go after it with a vengeance." This requires a principal who works with the staff and is good at getting teachers what they need to get the job done; the current principal does this well and is appreciated by the staff. As I walk through classrooms, I observe teachers walking through also, talking about students, and sharing ideas and teaching strategies.

*The Left Leg: Professionalism*

There may have been a time when Campbell Union School District was doing little professional development, but no more. No district within our region is doing more to guarantee that all teachers are implementing best practices in literacy than Campbell. Late afternoons, weekends, and summer days see rooms full of teachers learning best practice from trained professionals who are also experienced Campbell staff. Expert and peer coaching to support implementation of these practices are built into professional development activities.

When I talk with and observe teachers at Rosemary, I see consistent use of these best practices. What I also see, and teachers have commented on this to me, is continuity from classroom to classroom. Teachers are aware that what they are doing is building on what previous teachers did and will be built on by what future teachers do. Thus, the intellectual stimulation that results from collegiality and quality professional development, and the respect and voice in one's work life that comes from working with peers and administrators who respect you, leads to increased job satisfaction. These characteristics of a professional working environment are all an integral part of the Rosemary way.

Teachers do feel heard and respected by their principal and by the district office. The union representative told me that at the monthly union meetings, when reps from other schools raise school concerns, she very seldom has any issue to share.

Most telling was a comment from one experienced teacher about her experiences at Rosemary. When she started teaching many years ago, one veteran teacher approached her regularly and served as her mentor. Although her mentor retired several years ago, this teacher feels that she still looks over her shoulder for her mentor's support and approval. And more important, this teacher now seeks out beginning teachers at Rosemary and volunteers to be their mentor. As she said to me, "This is the Rosemary way, and I feel responsible to carry on the tradition."

Several other teachers who were part of this conversation agreed. Two teachers new to Rosemary shared how supportive they find the experienced teachers to be, and how different this was from the previous schools in which they had taught.

Over the last few years, San Jose State University (SJSU) has developed a collaborative working relationship with Campbell schools. Field placements in three preservice credential programs (concurrent multisubject/learning handicapped, 20 percent intern CLAD, and 100 percent intern) occur at Rosemary. SJSU offers support for the district program to support beginning teachers. In addition, four Rosemary staff members are enrolled in the Teacher Leadership Program, a school-based, action-research centered, MA program designed for teacher teams interested in becoming more effective school leaders without necessarily earning an administrative credential. I coordinate this master's program.

### The Arms: Managing and Leading Change

Change is clearly part of the Rosemary way, particularly change that is focused on doing what is right for students. When I asked teachers why the school was perceived to be special, they were not sure how to answer. Most often I heard about the great kids and parents, the trust, congeniality and collegiality among staff, the caring for the students, and caring about what's happening in each other's lives. Neither Harriet nor current teachers talk about the commanding presence of a long-term respected principal or a few teachers who led and enforced the Rosemary way. Yet, it is as Harriet says, "When teachers come, they don't do their thing. They do Rosemary's thing." The Rosemary thing means doing what is best for kids, and when that means change in current practice, then the Rosemary way is to change.

### The Heart: Resilience

If I heard one message most consistently that I think accounts for the deep commitment these teachers have to Rosemary and its students, it is that each teacher has chosen to teach at Rosemary, knowing that the student population is the most needy of any of the schools in Campbell. They sense that what they do every day is important, that the students need them, that the students and parents truly appreciate the teachers, that the littlest recognition is really appreciated by the students.

I had hoped to learn how Rosemary has stayed focused on doing what is best for students for so long. The answer is neither simple nor exportable. I think that the main lesson is that the elements of a resilient learning community are deeply enmeshed in the culture of Rosemary School; that is each student and each adult feels cared about, knows that the expectations are high and the support strong, and that his or her participation is valued by the community.

This is a school where I would happily send my grandchildren.

## Student Outcomes

Campbell Union School District (CUSD) assesses student progress based on district standards. At least 51 percent of all in students Grades two through eight are expected to score at or above the 50th percentile on the California Achievement Test (CAT) 5 for reading, language, and math; Spanish-speaking limited-English-proficient (LEP) students are assessed on the Spanish Assessment of Basic Education (SABE) 2. Clear minimal expectations by grade level have been set for district developed assessments in reading, writing, and mathematics. Data is reported by school and by grade within school for the CAT 5 and for the district assessment, with a composite score reported that indicates the percent of students at each school by grade level who meet or exceed district standards. Rosemary staff use this data to make decisions about their instructional practices. In addition, teacher judgment is a critical voice in decision making at Rosemary.

### District Standards

Fifty-one percent of Rosemary students meet or exceed the district standards for reading/language arts and 55 percent meet or exceed the district standards for mathematics. Results for Spanish-speaking LEP students were impressive—60 percent meet or exceed district standards for reading/language arts and 50 percent meet or exceed district standards for mathematics.

### Teacher Judgment

The clear focus for Rosemary School and CUSD overall is to have all students reading at grade level by the end of Grade three.

Books have been leveled, and teachers do regular alternate rankings of students to determine which students are at or above grade level, which students are making good progress and will reach grade level, and which students need increased support. The Rosemary principal reviews the alternate rankings with each teacher, Grades K–3, and helps the teacher plan for the increased support needed.

As I sat writing this section on January 29, 1998, I spent a half hour on the phone talking with the principal. She has recently completed the teacher conferences involved in this process and was able to tell me not only the number of students in each class who needed additional support, but talked with me at some length about the special circumstances of many individual children in order to explain to me how the process works. It is clear that teachers and the principal know students and their work well, and that the principal knows the teachers and their work well.

*Other Related Student Data*

The attendance rate at Rosemary is 95 percent, slightly above the district average. The student suspension rate is noticeably below the district average.

## Updates Written Winter 2006–2007 Rosemary School

In 1999 the academic performance index (API) schoolwide score for Rosemary was 511. In 2006 it was 669, a growth of 158 points. In 1999 the Hispanic students scored 410. In 2006 they averaged 631, a growth of 221 points. The school has demonstrated significant growth for students, especially for Hispanic students. So why is Rosemary a Program Improvement (PI) school under NCLB? In spite of the substantial improvement in student achievement, a huge "valued added," and the work of a dedicated faculty and a focused effort by the district, people come to Rosemary each day knowing that they have been identified as a "failing" school.

When people talk with me about the case studies after reading the first edition of this book, the first question they consistently ask is, "How is the Rosemary Way doing under NCLB?" I asked this question of teachers and the principal. Half of the teachers are new to Rosemary and the current principal is the third new principal, all since 1999. Yet, Harriet's words are still true: "When teachers come, they don't do their thing. They do Rosemary's thing."

I was asked by teachers to write about the negative impact NCLB has on the morale of a school and its community. Often teachers feel as if they are good people under siege. They feel that they take away too much instructional time for testing and test preparation. The related stress is one of the causes of the staff turnover. And, teachers said, as they did in 1998, that they will not give up on their students; they work hard; they love working with this community. Many of their students enter kindergarten never having held a pencil, not knowing any of the letters, not knowing how to spell their names, not speaking much English. It is estimated that only one-third attend preschool. By June, they are writing sentences, know all of their letters and numbers up to thirty, can write their names, and speak and have begun reading English. Teachers talked about how they support each other, visit each other's classrooms, and celebrate little successes as a community. Teachers send students with completed work to their previous teachers to celebrate their learning and growth. Teachers talked about the frustration and the exhaustion, but they also talked about the little miracles that keep them going. They talked about the need to help each student see the world of possibilities.

Teachers talked about working with the community to bring Halloween costumes, clothes, backpacks, and toys to the school for students and families. They also talked about teaching students the skills to be successful—they help students graph their results and set goals for improvement and involve students in designing rubrics for scoring their work. They talked about the positive outcomes that have come from a purposeful focus on English language development with their students.

I asked how they stop from excusing and enabling students due to their home situations, lack of English, and poverty. They told me that they do not give up because their students and parents do not give up. Unlike many other schools, Rosemary students and parents do not come with a sense of entitlement. Teachers are respected in the community. Many teachers indicated that most days at least one parent thanks them personally. They also talked about how teachers are not competitive with each other. They do not hoard resources and hide their best teaching practices. Sharing, mentoring, and coaching are still deeply embedded in the Rosemary Way.

I still think that I could happily send my grandchildren to Rosemary. At the same time, I have to wonder what positive outcome comes from labeling a school PI when it is so clear that the impact on student life and learning is so great!

## Rosemary School

401 West Hamilton Avenue
Campbell, CA 95008
408-364-4254
Web site: www.campbellusd.org

| Enrollment: | **448** |
|---|---|
| Hispanic | 78% |
| White (not Hispanic) | 7% |
| Vietnamese | 3% |
| African American | 6% |

| API | 1999* | 2005 | 2006 | Change |
|---|---|---|---|---|
| Total | 511 | 662 | 669 | +158 |
| Hispanic | 410 | 622 | 631 | +221 |
| White (not Hispanic) | 666 | NA* | NA* | |

\* not enough students in this category to be numerically significant

## Cesar Chavez

In 1999, the API schoolwide score for Cesar Chavez was 425. In 2006 it was 636, a growth of 211 points. In 1999 the Hispanic students scored 392. In 2006 they averaged 624, a growth of 232 points. The school has demonstrated significant growth for students, especially for Hispanic students. So why is Cesar Chavez a PI school under NCLB? In spite of the substantial improvement in student achievement, a huge "valued added," the work of a dedicated faculty and a focused effort by the district, and two awards from the San Jose Mayor's office for making substantial progress on student achievement, people come to Chavez each day knowing that they have been identified as a "failing" school.

At Chavez, as at Rosemary, I was asked by teachers to please write about the negative impact NCLB has on the morale of a school and its community. Only one teacher is still teaching at Chavez who was there in 1998. The school has had three additional principals in that time. Their concerns are the same as at Rosemary. In 2001, 75 percent of the Chavez students were being served in bilingual classrooms. In midyear, spring 2002, bilingual education was eliminated from the school. Many teachers became discouraged and left.

Teachers talked about respecting the student and parent's culture and language. In a community in which most parents speak Spanish at home, all communication, written and oral, is available in Spanish and English. No one is ever heard telling a student, "Stop speaking Spanish." Teachers talked with me about the need to teach students "education for life" and "to build habits of work." They have put in place a student recognition system used to reward students for displaying these habits, which include doing community service work, inviting other students to play, cleaning up the playground and cafeteria, and completing homework.

Several teachers and the principal talked about the neighborhood. In 1989 the neighborhood was gang infested. Due to a city, community, school-district initiative known as the Mayfair Initiative, the neighborhood is now safe. Many community agencies worked together to make this happen. Communication with the middle school located down the street has improved considerably. In fact, Mathson Middle School was highlighted in the November 2006 *California Educator* published by the California Teachers Association. Both schools worked together on a school uniform policy and articulation of programs has improved substantially.

Support is provided for teachers in the form of buddy teachers and resource teachers, and coaches are onsite for open court literacy and beginning teacher support. One teacher said that whenever she feels overwhelmed, someone steps up and volunteers to help.

I asked what impact NCLB has had on teaching. Cesar Chavez is in Alum Rock School District. The district-adopted curriculum is Open Court and Saxon Math, both controversial due to the structured lesson plans they require. One Chavez teacher said that this is "our curriculum. Open Court is not going away, and everyone is doing it. Attitude is everything. How can I use Open Court to be more effective?" Teachers recognize the value of having all teachers at a grade level doing the same thing, not only at Chavez but also throughout the district, especially given the high mobility of the student population. Another positive comment about NCLB is that looking at data has caused teachers to look deeply at the learning needs of individual students.

As I reread the original case study, many of the teacher quotes are still heard today. However, it is clear that the stress that comes from working with a student population from high-risk environments is very hard work. When a school demonstrates the progress students at Chavez have made over recent years, what purpose is served in labeling the school PI and sending a message of failure? Certainly, this is contrary to what it means to build a community that fosters resilience for its members.

## Cesar Chavez School

2000 Kammerer
San Jose, CA 95116
408-928-7300
Web site: www.arusd.org

**Enrollment:**          **663**

| | |
|---|---|
| Hispanic | 89.6% |
| White (not Hispanic) | 3.0% |
| African American | 6.0% |
| Pacific Islander | 2.0% |
| Filipino | 2.9% |
| Asian | 6.5% |

| API | 1999 | 2005 | 2006 | Change |
|---|---|---|---|---|
| Total | 425 | 635 | 636 | +211 |
| Hispanic | 392 | 628 | 624 | +232 |
| White (not Hispanic) | NA* | NA* | NA* | |

* not enough students in this category to be numerically significant

CHAPTER FIVE

# Providing High Expectations and Purposeful Support

*It is the first day of high school chemistry. Thirty-two stu-*
*dents wait expectantly for the teacher to speak. The teacher*
*begins the class by saying, "This is a college prep science*
*class. I have very high expectations. Look around you.*
*Based on past experience, I expect that only two of you will*
*earn A's in this class. Who will that be?"*

There were no A's in this class. I received one of the two B's. Let
no reader think that this is what I mean by high expectations.

Children need to be taught that strong habits of mind are
something they can learn through effort. It is the lesson of the little
engine that could—I think I can, I think I can, I think I can. . . until
she does.

One characteristic of a resilient learning community is that all
staff take collective responsibility for student learning—no blaming parents, students, administrators, the district office, the state
department of education, the tax payers. The educational community, including students and parents, come to see all students as
problem solvers, not problems to be solved. This requires taking

risks with and for students rather than labeling them at risk. This is the challenge that is at the very center of creating resilient learning communities. We need to look every student in the eye and say, "This work is important. You can do it. I won't give up on you. I am here to support you."

## TAKING THE EASY WAY OUT

Some teachers look at their student population and the socioeconomic problems they bring to school and at their own workload and expect too little of students and of themselves.

> The teacher who didn't help me at all in high school . . . was my computer lit. teacher. I got A's in that course. Just because he saw that I had A's, and that my name was all around the school for all the "wonderful things" I do, he just automatically assumed. He didn't really pay attention to who I was. The grade I think I deserved in that class was at least a C, but I got an A just because everybody else gave me A's. But everybody else gave me A's because I earned them. He gave me A's because he was following the crowd. He just assumed, "Yeah, well, she's a good student." And I showed up to class every day. He didn't help me at all because he didn't challenge me. Everybody else challenges me; I had to earn their grades. I didn't have to earn his grade. I just had to show up. (Nieto, 1996, p. 58)

> Spend an hour talking with each of the three students you identified in Chapter 1. Does each one of these students feel known within the school? Does each one feel that his or her work is known? Does each one feel that he or she is supported to meet high expectations?

How do students respond when they are not treated with the respect that comes from knowing them and their work well, when they are treated as if they are not capable of using their minds and hearts well? They drop out emotionally, intellectually, and physically. Ted Sizer (1996) spent a day shadowing a high school student named Martha. At the end of the day, she suddenly hissed into Sizer's ear, "I am not stupid, I am not stupid, I am not stupid (p. 132). How many students feel not known and stupid?

# HIGH EXPECTATIONS: FOCUS ON LITERACY

Emmy Werner found that effective reading skills by grade four was one of the most potent predictors of successful adult adaptation. It is certainly true that students who are not reading at grade level when they begin grade four typically struggle throughout the rest of their school careers.

Increasingly, thanks in part to the high-stakes accountability measures in NCLB, many elementary schools are focusing on student literacy as their most important academic priority. For many years, academicians argued about the correct way to teach literacy. Journals are full of articles arguing that all students learn best with a program stressing skills (phonetics typically), while others argued for whole language (literature). We now know that best practice is a strong combination of both and that the emphasis should vary depending on the learning needs and learning style of the individual student. Best practice is clearly based on teachers knowing individual students and their work well.

# HIGH EXPECTATIONS: HABITS OF MIND

Schools that expect all students to use their minds and hearts well focus on asking questions of students and adults, the answering of which requires challenging one's mind. Central Park East Secondary School (CPESS) in East Harlem is well known for this. Students are consistently asked the following questions:

| | |
|---|---|
| Evidence: | How do we know what we know? |
| Viewpoint: | Who's speaking? |
| Connections: | What causes what? |
| Suppositions: | How might things have been different? |
| Relevance: | Who cares? |

In order to graduate from CPESS, students must complete fourteen exhibitions. These five questions are formed into a rubric for graduation committees to use as they judge student work and guide the questions committee members ask in order to clarify and extend the student's learning. In addition, these questions are posted in all classrooms and are at the heart of the curriculum in every class. They are used in all classrooms, in discipline conferences, and, based on my observations when I visited CPESS, are often used by students as they talk with their peers in cooperative learning groups and with their friends in the hallways. The purposeful focus on these five questions—habits of mind—demonstrates to every student that they are expected to use their minds and hearts well, and when students demonstrate that these habits of mind are an integral part of how they think and act, they are demonstrating their abilities to do so.

Remember from Chapter 1 that Anzar High School is also guided by its habits of mind (EPERRs, Figure 1.3) and graduation exhibitions. So are many other schools that are affiliated with the Coalition of Essential Schools (www.essentialschools.org).

Teaching to habits of mind requires teaching with a rigor that is both beyond that expected in most classrooms and beyond what most adults expect of ourselves. It requires a fundamental change in what teachers expect of students and of themselves. Habits of teaching and learning are deeply rooted. Schools will become very different institutions only if we are very serious about the need to change our fundamental expectations and if we are willing to stick with it over a long period of time.

Wouldn't it be wonderful if all school was like kindergarten. As described by Debbie Meier (1995),

> Kindergarten is the one place—maybe the last place—where teachers are expected to know children well, even if they don't hand in their homework, finish their Friday tests, or pay attention. Kindergarten teachers know children by listening and looking. They know that learning is personalized because kids are incorrigibly idiosyncratic. . . . Kindergarten teachers know that helping children learn to become more self-reliant is part of their task—starting with tying shoes and going to the bathroom. Catering to children's growing independence is a natural part of a kindergarten teacher's classroom life. This is, alas, the last time children are given independence, encouraged to make choices, and allowed to move about on their own steam. (p. 48)

## WHAT GETS IN THE WAY?

Belief systems that suggest that using one's mind and heart well is for only certain students, and practices that reinforce this belief, must be addressed if schools are to be built around the protective factors of resilience. The way schools track and group students by perceived abilities tells students what's expected of them. These labels become self-fulfilling prophecies for far too many of our children. Too often children see the labels as a deterrent to try. Too often, teachers use the labels as an excuse to not challenge anyone but the most motivated to use their minds and hearts well. As Debbie Meier says, children find themselves driven into dumbness by a failure to challenge their curiosity, to build on their natural drive toward competence.

It is common for children of color and of poverty to be labeled as needy and at risk, for them to be placed in remedial and special education classrooms year after year, for academic expectations to be low, and for few students to graduate from high school and attend college.

One might think that labeling and tracking would be most common in inner-city schools. Many of our most affluent schools define academic winners and losers through a complex tracking system, however. Students know what it means to be a red bird or a blue bird or a yellow bird. They know what it means to be in the X class, or the Y class, or the Z class. They know the difference between AP, honors, college prep, general, and remedial. They also know that, for many students, where they are placed has far less to do with ability than with motivation or how actively one's parents are involved in the school. Thus, many middle-class students know being academically challenged is optional.

Tracking is perhaps the most controversial issue for schools today. When the parents of "academic" students do not feel that their children are being appropriately challenged, they complain loudly. They have a right to complain; their students—all students—should be intellectually challenged in school. These parents are often involved with the school through various school committees. They know and are school board members. They are most likely to remove their students to private schools and increasingly to charter schools. In addition, given the reality of schools today—large schools, large class sizes, privacy of teaching practice, lack of resources, poor professional development practices—the vast majority of schools and, in particular, most teachers are not prepared to challenge all their students, particularly not in a heterogeneous classroom setting. Mandating heterogeneous classes will not improve student achievement. Major systemic reform is necessary if high expectations are truly going to be the focus of schooling for all students.

## WHAT ELSE GETS IN THE WAY?

Another thing that gets in the way is not practicing what we say we believe, and therefore searching for easy answers for complex problems. I offer two examples.

The first has to do with recognizing and rewarding that which we say we value.

- Many schools write a mission statement that includes students demonstrating their abilities to work cooperatively. Yet, when I visit schools, I notice bulletin boards recognizing "the student of the month" and "the employee of the month," both very clear statements that the work of a very limited number of individuals working independently is valued. Wouldn't it be more consistent and beneficial to recognize lots of people for the work they do together toward meeting the mission of the school?
- School and school district goals listed under the mission statement are usually related to academic learning. Yet, if we look at what most schools recognize most publicly, it is the athletic program and social events. Winning sports teams, cheerleaders, and dances receive far more recognition than achievements related to where students spend most of time—in classrooms.

Second, and again tied to most school-district mission and goal statements, is the stated desire for all students to be proactive problem solvers.

- Yet, when I visit schools, I notice that the primary instructional strategy employed in most classrooms is teacher-led instruction. The research on brain compatible learning has become quite well known, and yet the instructional model remains the same—"teaching as telling"—teachers working with large groups of students. The message to students is clear: I am not expected to work very hard; the teacher does the hard work not me; I just need to memorize enough to get by; my interests and my mind and, in fact me, are not valued at this school.

- Many schools claim to use site-based decision making. However, important decisions regarding budget, hiring, curriculum scope and sequences, and textbook adoption are still made primarily by the principal or district office or by teachers privately in their classrooms. Even when teachers are collaboratively involved in some decision making, parents and students are too often left out. If students are to learn to be proactive problem solvers—to develop the habits of mind to use their minds and hearts well—the school needs to demonstrate this value in the classroom and throughout the school community.

## HIGH EXPECTATIONS MEANS BELIEVING THAT ALL STUDENTS ARE CAPABLE OF USING THEIR MINDS AND HEARTS WELL

Fostering resilience means that teachers are "in kids' faces," knowing them and their work well, expecting all students to meet high expectations and telling them so. As Gary Bloom, associate director of the New Teacher Center and former superintendent of schools for Aromas-San Juan Unified (Anzar High School) says, "Teachers need to be relentless in insuring that students follow through and experience small successes; they phone parents; they harass and harangue; they don't give up; they advocate relentlessly for students. It needs to be more work for a student to fail than it is to get onboard."

Students who need academic support are accelerated (helped to catch up), rather than remediated (too often associated with falling further behind). Only when we have high expectations and purposeful support for our students will all students have a sense of the future that is optimistic and hopeful. This requires that teachers and administrators believe, say, and practice for all students: "This work is important. You can do it. I won't give up on you. I am here to support you."

## PURPOSEFUL SUPPORT

It is important that purposeful support be designed very specifically to help students stay challenged to use their minds and hearts well and to provide safety nets for those students who need additional support to do so. Please do not think that having one or a few of the following examples means the school is a resilient learning community. Purposeful support is important, but only one part of the protective factors. Caring, high expectations and purposeful support, and participation should pervade all aspects of the school.

> Think about your three students. What support is in place within their school to help assure that they acquire strong habits of mind?

## WHAT WOULD A SCHOOL LOOK LIKE WHOSE CULTURE IS CENTERED ON HIGH EXPECTATIONS AND PURPOSEFUL SUPPORT?

- Reasonable, positive, public, known, and consistently enforced policies and procedures are in place. Optimally, students are involved in drafting, evaluating, and revising these policies.
- The campus is well maintained with little litter and graffiti.
- A broad range of student work is on display throughout the school.
- Teachers are heard talking about individual students and their work and ways to proactively support that student's learning.
- Every student can name at least two adults who know him or her well and his or her work well.
- Students are seen working together on school projects.
- Students are seen tutoring other students inside and outside the classroom.
- The parent's and extended family's roles in supporting student learning are valued and supported through parent and grandparent workshops, a parent library, and the availability of social services support. Such roles are also

supported by proactively seeking and utilizing the knowledge and skills of the family as a resource in the school, in the classroom, and in the curriculum.

- Members of the community are seen mentoring students. Research by the Public/Private Ventures in Philadelphia found that kids enrolled in Big Brothers and Big Sisters were percent less likely to skip school than a matched control group, 33 percent less likely to exhibit violent behavior, and 46 percent less likely to try drugs for the first time. Enrolled African American youth were 70 percent less likely to try drugs (Butler, 1997).
- Programs proven to support student achievement and sense of belonging (i.e., Advancement Via Individual Determination [AVID; www.avidonline.org], Link Crew [www.linkcrew.com], Reading Recovery [www.reading recovery.org], Asset Development [www.search-institute. org], Tribes are highly visible on campus.
- Teachers, parents, and students talk openly about the commitment of the principal and district to all students learning to use their minds and hearts well.
- Staff articulate a common mission that all agree transcends personal differences.

## WHAT WOULD CURRICULUM, INSTRUCTION, AND ASSESSMENT BE LIKE IN A SCHOOL THAT IS DESIGNED TO FOSTER HIGH EXPECTATIONS AND PURPOSEFUL SUPPORT FOR ALL STUDENTS?

### Curriculum

- Students are actively engaged in interdisciplinary, thematic, project-based work that is based on a limited number of important content standards.
- Projects have significance to students and are based on important questions raised by students, teachers, and community members.
- Curriculum respects and acknowledges the ethnography and community of the students, using this as a departure

point for curriculum that explores diversity of culture and opinion within and without the community.

- Teachers differentiate curriculum that addresses learning styles and special needs of students.
- Students comment (or proudly complain) that the work is challenging and takes time.

## Instruction

- Classes are heterogeneously grouped for most of the day, with regrouping as appropriate.
- Students usually are working in small groups or independently.
- There are well-defined safety net in place to accelerate students who are falling behind in their academic progress. Students are required to participate in these safety nets in order to accelerate their learning. Safety nets are regularly evaluated for their effectiveness.
- When teachers ask questions, students are required to use higher-order thinking skills to answer and all students have equal access to respond; when students ask questions, teachers usually reply with a question that requires thought by the student, rather than with the answer.
- Teachers differentiate instruction to address the need of all students.

## Assessment

- Student learning is assessed in a variety of ways, including the use of well-publicized rubrics, public exhibitions, and self-reflection by students.

> Rate your own school or schools you know well using the checklist. Which are strengths for your school and what are the areas of concern?

- Individual teachers use assessment strategies on a daily basis to diagnose the learning of individual students and to adjust and differentiate instruction based on this assessment.
- Teachers review student work and other assessment data together to guide school and classroom practice.
- When asked, students talk articulately about their best work.

# WHAT DO TEACHER AND ADMINISTRATOR ROLES LOOK LIKE IN SUCH A SCHOOL?

- The principal knows students and student work well and is often seen engaged in conversations with teachers about individual students and their learning.
- The principal knows students and student work well and is often seen engaged in conversations with students about their learning.
- Teachers and school and district administrators have agreed on best practices in a limited number of areas of focus (literacy, habits of mind), and time, resources, and professional development are supporting implementation—including expert and peer coaching and collaborative-action research.
- Time is provided for teachers to discuss the needs and successes of individual students.

> Rate your own school or schools you know well using the checklist. Which are strengths for your school and what are the areas of concern?

- Time is provided for teachers to review student work and other school data together and discuss implications of this data for improving classroom practice.
- Teachers talk openly about how supportive the principal and district are regarding supporting ideas and helping to provide resources.
- Teachers seek out parents as partners in supporting the learning of students and, in particular, contact parents regularly when students are doing well.

# ONCE AGAIN, DOES IT MATTER WHICH SCHOOL A CHILD ATTENDS?

IT DOES MATTER! We know what works in schools, and we can and are creating such schools. (Darling-Hammond, 1997; Marzano, 2003) The three schools described in the following case studies are small schools that opened in 2004 within the Alum Rock School District in San Jose, California. Along with Dennis

Chaconas, I have served as the coach for these schools, beginning with supporting the design teams that wrote the original proposals and serving on the district task force that wrote the board small schools policy.

The teachers and administrators at these three schools are relentless in their support/demand that all students learn to use their minds and hearts well.

# CASE STUDY: ALUM ROCK SMALL SCHOOLS OF CHOICE

## Written Winter 2006–2007

It is June 2003. I am attending a parent meeting at a church in the Alum Rock School District in east San Jose. There are approximately three hundred parents and three school board members present. Almost all parents are Spanish speaking. Parents are asking the board to support the opening of small schools of choice. The response is for the most part positive. The parents have been organized by People Acting in Community Together (PACT, www.pactsj.org), a community group affiliated with the PICO National Network. A new superintendent has been hired by Alum Rock, and he will begin work in a few weeks. I was invited due to my position as director of the LEAD Center (www.leadces.com).

Over the next few months, three design teams began to write proposals to open new schools. Each design team consisted of teachers and parents, with a PACT community organizer, Dennis Chaconas, and me coaching the teams. The new superintendent supported this initiative. In November, the board approved a new policy allowing this work to commence. By spring, all three proposals were approved and the work began to recruit students and teachers, to decide where the new schools would be located, and to prepare for the openings in September 2004.

The work was difficult. The new superintendent left early in the 2004 school year. Teachers and principals at the large schools were threatened by the possible success and student recruitment for the new small schools. The three small schools shared campuses with three larger schools and were not necessarily welcomed. For many people working in maintenance and operations, business services, and human resources, any work required to open the new schools was on top of an already full load. There were no procedures in place to make this work a priority. The district plan for curriculum and instruction called for schools to use Open Court and Saxon Math, but the three new schools by board policy were to have autonomy; the role of the District Curriculum Department was therefore not clear. The unions were very protective of their contracts and were suspicious of waivers that the small schools requested. And, the relationship between PACT and district administration was strained based on previous conflicts over how to engage parents in the workings of the schools.

The schools did open. A year later, when the state tests scores were released, it was clear that the students at the new schools had done well in Year 1.

In spring 2005, the board voted to not approve two additional small school proposals. The reason given was that the district needed time to look at long-term facility priorities. Relations with PACT and the district worsened. In spring 2006, the interim superintendent and deputy superintendent (soon to be appointed superintendent) announced long-term facility plans for the three small schools. All three schools would be moved from their current locations and placed on other school sites. Parents, administrators, and teachers at the small schools raised concerns that the new locations were distant from the current locations. The district promised transportation for at least the first year and argued convincingly that the new locations would allow for continuing expansion of the three schools as described in their implementation plans. District support during Year 3 has been good.

When the state test scores were released for the second year, it was clear that the three small schools had done very well. LUCHA (Learning in an Urban Community with High Achievement) was the top scoring school in the district and Renaissance was the top scoring middle school and placed third overall. Adelante had perhaps the most amazing results. Adelante is a dual immersion school enrolling Grades K–2 in 2005–2006 and teaches exclusively in Spanish except for an hour of English language development each day. Second graders at Adelante scored at the district average. See the following school data.

## Learning in an Urban Community With High Achievement (LUCHA)

LUCHA's mission statement states that "LUCHA is a place where empowered students, united with invested parents and families, a relentless staff, and the greater community, construct academic, social, and personal achievement to be conscientious leaders now and in the future." There is an intense focus on language arts and math standards, while incorporating project-based learning and extending the classroom through service learning, field trips, family meetings, and positive community input.

Three brief snapshots help describe LUCHA:

- Each day begins with a school meeting on the blacktop. Students line up with their classmates and teachers. They recite the school pledge: "We are LUCHA leaders. . . ." They pledge allegiance, sing songs and hear the daily announcements. They walk proudly to their classrooms. Many parents stay for this meeting when they drop their students off in the morning. The focus on each student being a leader is a consistent theme at the school. The partnership with parents is also a consistent theme.
- Every teacher uses Open Court and Saxon Math as his or her base curriculum. Teachers also have agreed-upon ten essential learning standards at each grade for language arts and ten for math that they expect every student to master. They call them "big hairy audacious goals." Teachers have written formative assessments for each of these standards at each grade level. They use student data to inform practice on a regular basis, plan for student interventions, and reteach as necessary. All teachers also develop grade-level Understanding by Design (Wiggins & McTighe, 1998) units for social studies and science that reinforce the essential learning standards as well as meet state content standards. The principal is visible in classrooms every day, knows all students and parents by name, and holds teachers accountable to meet the high expectations that the school has for every student.
- At the end-of-the-year evening celebration, every student receives a certificate of accomplishment from his or her teacher. Every parent who has met the thirty-hour volunteer expectation receives a certificate. At the June 2006

celebration, 95 percent of the parents were recognized. My observation was that parents were at least as proud as their students.

## Renaissance Academy for Arts, Science, and Social Justice

Renaissance's mission statement states that "Renaissance is a place for students to grow the educational roots that will feed their minds and to dream the dreams that will sustain their spirit. But what good is the best education in the world if you remain blind and unconcerned about injustice on your doorstep? Reaching our potential involves making the world a better place."

Renaissance opened with Grade six in 2004, added Grade seven in 2005, and added Grade eight in 2006. In 2006 the initial principal left to become the principal at a large middle school in Alum Rock. She was asked to work with the teachers at that school to personalize the school into small learning communities. Renaissance was relocated over the summer, and its new location is on the campus with their former principal. The new principal, although new to Renaissance, is committed to small schools and has been well received by the Renaissance teachers and parents, many of whom were involved in his hiring process.

Three brief snapshots will help describe Renaissance:

- Grade-level teaming and advisories are at the heart of the school. Teachers loop. The initial teachers who opened the school in 2004 teaching and advising sixth graders, taught and advised the same students as seventh graders in 2005–2006, and are now teaching and advising the same students as eighth graders in 2006–2007. Likewise, the teachers hired in 2005 to teach sixth graders are teaching seventh graders this year. Thus, students and families are well known. And, teachers know each other very well. They support each other as teachers, and they support each other with their students. An important component of the advisory is the student-led conferences during which students lead the conversation with their parents and advisor regarding the progress they are making in school. These conferences occur twice a year for all students and one additional time for any students with a GPA under 2.0.

- Interventions are in place such that all students know that they are expected to learn at high levels. Teachers are paid to operate homework centers before and after school. Two days a week in advisories, students are grouped homogeneously by learning needs and receive focused tutoring. Afterschool all-stars provide homework support, enrichment activities, and athletics for eighty students each day. All-star staff maintains close communication with teachers and parents regarding homework completion and behavior.

- In September 2006, Dennis Chaconas and I asked the new principal, "How would a visitor know you are a school focused on social justice by visiting your classrooms? What evidence makes you different?" He brought our questions to the teachers. Two of the teachers are enrolled in the San Jose State master's program in collaborative leadership. As they wrote in a paper for that class, "We were brainstorming ways we could incorporate a social justice piece into our curriculum and make it meaningful for our students. We thought a simulation would be the best way to jumpstart the social justice curriculum and get students' hearts and minds fired up on issues of racism, sexism, and inequality. Through this process, we hoped to teach students to use their hearts and minds well." They organized a simulation much like the well-known blue/brown eye simulation done in a classroom in the 1950s. They took their proposal to the Renaissance faculty, and after several discussions, everyone agreed to participate. Parents were notified, with a full explanation that the purpose was to help students understand racism. The simulation lasted seven days. Some students were labeled as "bunnies" and others as "kittens." The bunnies were treated with fewer privileges than the kittens. Considerable attention was given to using advisory time to debrief, including discussing various aspects of racism such as Jim Crow laws, the civil rights movement, the Holocaust, and the Trail of Tears. Feedback from students and parents has been very positive.

- Academic exhibitions are held each trimester. For the month before these exhibitions, students choose a topic, research it, and develop oral and written presentations. The fall 2006 exhibition included work on poetry, earthquakes, Sumerian ziggurats, and statistics to name a few projects. Self-expression takes more forms than oral and written presentations! During the winter trimester, students assemble a performance exhibition featuring singing, dancing, poetry reading, and drama presentations and feature their own "incomparable" jazz band. These are evening events.

## Adelante

The mission of Adelante is "for all students to achieve high levels of bilingual proficiency and multicultural competency through a rigorous English and Spanish dual-language immersion instruction program. Our school philosophy is based on the belief that, El que sabe dos idiomas vale por dos (one who knows two languages is worth two)."

Adelante opened as a K–1 school in 2004, added Grade two in 2005, added Grade three in 2006, and will eventually be K–8. The design team, six or more teachers and fifteen or more parents, met every Friday night for months preparing the initial proposal. Being involved in a dual-immersion school, using a The 90/10 instructional model, was a long time dream of the teachers who involved themselves in the design and opening of this school. The 90/10 model means that, in Grades K–1, 90 percent of the instruction is in Spanish and 10 percent in English, and the percentages switch in later grades, 50/50 by Grade five. The design requires that approximately half of students be English speakers and half be Spanish speakers. All teachers must be fluent Spanish speakers well trained to teach in this way.

Three brief snapshots will help describe Adelante:

- As at LUCHA, each day begins with a school meeting on the blacktop. Students recite the school pledge: "Hoy es un dia nuevo . Hoy creo en mi mismo. . . ." They pledge allegiance, sing songs, and hear the daily announcements. This, of course, is done in Spanish. Many parents stay for this meeting after they drop off their students in the morning.
- Last March, I attended a staff meeting. Each teacher brought two lists showing assessment results for his or her students in

five academic areas: word fluency, writing, spelling, comprehension, and vocabulary. One list showed the results for each student for January 2006 and the other for March 2006. Teachers color-coded the results according to students' meeting or not meeting standard in each area. One teacher started the conversation by reviewing her results. The principal and other teachers asked questions. The teacher talked about who had met standard and what she was doing for each student who had not. They talked about the increasing number of students at or above standard and, given that the standards are harder to meet each quarter, how students would be supported to meet the higher standard by June. Then a second teacher presented. I was "awed" by the honesty and openness of these conversations and how well each teacher and the principal knew each student. This conversation happens quarterly at Adelante.

- At the end of the school year, Adelante holds a graduation for kindergarten students. Forty-five 6-year-olds dress in caps and gowns and march into the multipurpose room. The room is full of family members. Each student comes to the microphone, and, in Spanish, says his or her name and what he or she is planning to do as a career. The commitment to creating a college-going culture is very strong. The pride among the whole educational community is humbling.

## Commonalities Across the Three Schools

- All students, staff and parents are known well.
- Expectations for all students, staff, and parents are high.
- Interventions are focused and purposeful.
- Student data drives instructional practice.
- Students demonstrate their learning in multitude ways, including regular exhibitions of their work.
- The top-ten list of essential content standards guides curriculum planning.
- Teacher and parent voices are central to decision making
- A strong college-going culture is highly visible.

## Final Word

*What We Know*

Students learn best when they are known well, when expectations are high and support is focused and purposeful, and when their voices and the voices of their parents are valued.

Teachers teach best when they are known well, when expectations are high and support is focused and purposeful, and when their voices are valued.

Schools work best when these conditions are in place for students, parents, and educators.

*Theory of Action*

Powerful teaching and learning requires skillful, committed teachers and administrators who focus on a limited number of essential learning standards, use a broad diversity of student data to guide teaching and learning on a daily basis, and work with students in a respectful way that holds themselves and every student accountable to master these standards.

**LUCHA**
1250 S. King RD
San Jose, CA 95122
408-928-8300

**Renaissance**
1720 Hopkins Dr.
San Jose, CA 95122
408-928-1950

**Adelante**
299 Ridgemont AVE
San Jose, CA 95127
408-928-1900
Web site: www.arusd.org

**Enrollment:**

| **LUCHA** | **227** |
|---|---|
| Hispanic | 87.5% |
| White (not Hispanic) | 2.0% |
| African American | 5.0% |
| Asian | 3.0% |
| Filipino | 2.0% |

| **Renaissance** | **205** |
|---|---|
| Hispanic | 75.0% |
| White (not Hispanic) | 10.0% |
| Asian | 4.7% |
| American Indian or Alaska Native | 0.6% |
| Filipino | 5.9% |
| African American | 3.8% |

| **Adelante** | **100** |
|---|---|
| Hispanic | 94.0% |
| White (not Hispanic) | 1.0% |
| Asian | 3.0% |
| Filipino | 1.0% |
| African American | 1.0% |

| API | 2005 * | 2006 | Change |
|---|---|---|---|
| LUCHA | 753 | 834 | +81 |
| Renaissance | 736 | 769 | +33 |
| Adelante | NA* | 692 | |

* no students enrolled in Grades two and beyond

CHAPTER SIX

# I Value Your Participation

*Now Sit Down and Shut Up*

*When one has no stake in the way things are, when one's needs or opinions are provided no forum, when one sees oneself as the object of unilateral actions, it takes no particular wisdom to suggest that one would rather be elsewhere.*

—Sarason, 1990, p. 83

Stated in a more positive way:

*When people have an opportunity to participate in decisions and shape strategies that vitally affect them, they will develop a sense of ownership in what they have determined and commitment to seeing that the decisions are sound and the strategies are useful, effective and carried out. This theory is basic to a democratic society.*

—Burns & Lofquist, 1996, p. 10

Given the constraints I placed on you, it is likely that you have few if any memories to write down. You may remember a field trip, or the learning that followed the death of a fellow student or public figure, or learning in a few select classes. Most likely you remember little that was directly part of the academic curriculum in high school. If I do not place these limitations on you, however, you probably have a flood of positive and negative memories, many deeply felt and often reminisced about, that are of great significance to you.

I have asked hundreds of people to do this task. Typically, in a group of thirty, no more than five have anything written down at the end. Yet, all thirty have vivid memories of participating in sports, marching band, or dances, attending sporting events and pep rallies, laughing about the idiosyncrasies of particular teachers and fellow students, and being laughed at or excluded by fellow students. No wonder so many taxpayers are hesitant to vote for additional taxes for schools. Their memories indicate that what was learned in classrooms was not particularly important to their lives. Most people do not feel that the academics of school actively engaged them or challenged them to use their minds or hearts well. Most people feel that the academics of school were "done to them" with little consideration for their interests and with little knowledge of who they were as people.

> Think about your high school years. What are your most powerful and valuable memories? It doesn't matter whether these are positive or negative. You should have several examples in mind. Eliminate any that involved athletics, the fine and performing arts, school leadership activities, and school social life. Focus only on memories from academic classes. Next, and harder to do, eliminate the memory if it is primarily associated with the charisma of the teacher. Write down whatever you still have in mind.

## PARTICIPATION AS THE THIRD PROTECTIVE FACTOR

The need to have control over one's life, to participate in how one spends one's days, is a fundamental human need. The challenge for a school that is striving to foster resilience is to engage all students in powerful learning activities and in meaningful roles, while helping them build the skills necessary to succeed at these activities and roles. This does not and should not require special programs or elaborate elective classes. It does require that teachers know students and their work well. It does require that the teacher allow students to be the workers and the teacher to be "the guide on the side" rather than "the sage on the stage." Basic skills are not neglected in such a school. Basic skills are learned and taught because they are needed to deal with the issues and projects that form the core of the instructional program. And all students are expected and purposefully supported to participate in these learning experiences.

Returning to Bonnie Benard's quote that opens Chapter 3, we can create this kind of school if and only if the practices we want for the students are also in place for the adults. Thus, the principal must value the active participation of teachers, parents, classified staff, community, and students in meaningful ways in the workings of the school.

> Talk with your three students again. How engaged are they in what happens in their classes and in the life of the school? What impact do they feel they have on the school?
>
> Talk with three teachers and three classified staff members. How engaged do they feel they are in what happens in the life of the school? Talk with the principal. How engaged is the principal in what happens in classrooms and in the district? What impact do these teachers, classified staff, and principal feel they have on the school?

Going one step further, the superintendent and school board must model this behavior and value the meaningful participation of site administrators, teachers, parents, classified staff, community, and students in meaningful ways in the workings of the individual schools and the district as a whole. The climate and culture established by district leadership plays a major role in determining the climate and culture of individual schools. I honestly believe that one cannot truly improve and sustain reform one school at a time, a theory of action behind many school reform initiatives. Coherence with the district and skillful districtwide leadership are necessary if schools are to truly improve and sustain that improvement. The case studies in Chapter 2 and 3 are meant to demonstrate this point.

# WHAT WOULD A SCHOOL LOOK LIKE WHOSE CULTURE IS CENTERED ON MEANINGFUL PARTICIPATION BY ALL STUDENTS?

## Two Examples

Ann Cook, the director of Urban Academy, one of the small public high schools in New York City and a Coalition of Essential Schools Mentor School, designed the physical environment of the school to clearly encourage, almost require, that students and teachers participate together in daily dialog outside the classroom. All teachers share a common faculty office. Their desks are in close proximity to one another, and, as a result, teachers are often talking about school practices. Student lockers are located in this faculty office or in the adjoining room, causing students to be present for many of these discussions. In a conversation with Ann, she shared that this was a premeditated decision designed to encourage just such interactions. For schools to be successful, teachers must have the opportunity to talk regularly. If students are to learn to use their minds well, they need to be engaged in listening to and participating in discussions with adults that require and model the mind being used well (www.urbanacademy.org).

Souhegan High School in Amherst, New Hampshire, is governed by a community council composed of a majority of students. The council consists of approximately two administrators, ten teachers, six parents, and twenty-four students. Half of the students are elected by their peers, and half are appointed through a recruitment and application process designed to assure that a wide range of student groups are represented on the council. When I visited Souhegan in the spring of 1997, the principal said that he had never overridden a decision of the council, even when the council voted for a new bell schedule that the faculty was divided over. When I contacted the school again in 2006, I was told by the current principal that the practice is still alive and well (www.sprise.com/shs).

As was true in Chapters 4 and 5, what follows are things that I look for when I visit a school. Many of the items included in Chapter 4 or in Chapter 5 could fit here as well; several are repeated. In fact, many of the ideas listed in Chapter 5 as support (i.e., tutoring) are appropriate here as valued participation (i.e., the value for the tutor). As in the previous chapters, no item on this list is sacred. The one sacred premise remains the belief in the potential of all students to learn the habits of mind to use their minds and hearts well. Again, building a resilient learning community requires major shifts in the belief systems, culture, and daily practice of most schools; this is not an easy fix.

- Students are working in the library, computer lab, laboratories, and hallways, individually and collaboratively with peers.
- Students are engaged in required helpfulness.
- Older students are seen working with younger students.
- Students are engaged with peers as peer helpers, conflict resolvers, and tutors.
- Students spend time each week in service learning projects on and off campus.
- Class meetings and schoolwide forums are held regularly to gather student input regarding meaningful school issues. These meetings are often facilitated by students.
- An effort is being made to include all student groups in the daily life of the school; students are not seen on the fringes of the school campus, alienated and voicing displeasure with the school, staff, and peers.
- A large percentage of the students participate in and lead a wide range of school activities.
- Signs on campus encourage students to join activities and do not indicate hurdles to complete; the words "students must" do not appear on school postings.
- Time is provided at least weekly for teachers to work together on curriculum, instruction, and assessment.
- Most students, faculty, and staff are known and welcomed by name, and many parents and community members are known and welcomed by name.
- Drug, alcohol, smoking, and fighting infractions are statistically small and show an annual decrease.

# WHAT WOULD CURRICULUM, INSTRUCTION, AND ASSESSMENT BE LIKE IN A SCHOOL DESIGNED TO FOSTER MEANINGFUL PARTICIPATION BY ALL STUDENTS?

## Curriculum

- Curriculum is project based, set around complex issues, some of which relate to school and community issues.
- Student work is posted throughout the school.
- Students have choices in the specifics of what they investigate, how they do the investigation, and how they demonstrate what they have learned.
- Service learning is a part of every student's academic program.

## Instruction

- Teachers ask students questions that require students to do critical, reflective thinking, that is, the questions associated with Anzar and CPESS's habits of mind.

> Rate your own school or schools you know well using the checklist. Which are strengths for your school and what are the areas of concern?

- Teachers spend much of their time coaching students, and students spend much of their time working individually and in small groups.
- Students are actively engaged in lessons; they are not seen sitting unengaged in the back of classrooms.
- School resources are readily available; computers and resource materials are easy for students to access.

## Student Assessment

- Students exhibit and reflect on what they have learned.
- Standards for quality work are well known, and often designed with student input. Rubrics are created jointly by teachers and students.
- Teachers use student work to guide classroom and school practices.

- Student exhibitions are regularly shared within the school and community.

## MORE DETAILS ON CURRICULUM, INSTRUCTION, AND ASSESSMENT

Readers of the first edition have asked me for more specifics on curriculum, instruction, and assessment. Numerous books have been written on these topics, of course, and details are beyond the scope of this book.

Briefly however, the focus should be on answering the following three questions:

- What do we want students to understand, know, and be able to do? (Essential Outcomes)
- How will we know that they understand, know, and/or are able to do these things? (Common Assessments)
- What will we do when they do not learn it? (Support)

I am a strong believer in Understanding by Design (UbD) and differentiated instruction (see McTighe & Wiggins, 2004; Tomlinson & McTighe, 2006; Wiggins & McTighe, 1998).

In addition, most states have generated long lists of content standards for each subject area for each grade. Teachers cannot and will not teach to long lists in a way that allows students to actively engage in learning—in ways that teach students to use their minds and hearts well. Districts should engage teachers, working across grade levels, in selecting the most important content standards, sometimes called power standards—perhaps ten for language arts and ten for math at each grade level and articulated backward from grade level to grade level—and designing curriculum maps, formative assessments, and interventions around these standards. The small schools described in Chapter 5 are doing this.

## WHAT DO TEACHER AND ADMINISTRATOR ROLES LOOK LIKE IN SUCH A SCHOOL?

- Principals, teachers, students, parents, community members, and classified staff are engaged in schoolwide decision making around issues of substance, including establishing school priorities, budgeting to support those priorities, and hiring of personnel.
- Norms for decision making, consensus building, and conflict resolution are mutually agreed upon, followed, and regularly reassessed.
- Meetings focus on meaningful input and decision making rather than information giving; agendas are posted with opportunities for agenda input; relevant information is provided ahead of meetings; participants arrive at meetings on time; meetings start on time and end on time.
- Divergent thinking is encouraged and heard in formal meetings and in informal conversations.
- Conversations and comments reflect respect for others, in and out of meetings. Put downs, side conversations, and comments that indicate exclusion are not heard in or out of meetings.
- Mistakes are celebrated as learning experiences, and responsibility for mistakes are shared without blame.
- Teachers work collegially, sharing curriculum and instructional strategies, talking about students and student work, coaching each other to be more effective. Time and resources are provided to support this.
- Teachers talk freely about feeling valued by administrators, staff, parents, and students as participants in the whole school community.
- Administrators, faculty, classified staff, students, and parents seem to enjoy being together; across roles, people seek each other out, talk together, and laugh together.
- Faculty and staff are not seen complaining, blaming, or brooding in the faculty room or in the parking lot.
- Students are given classroom and schoolwide responsibilities of increasing importance with age.

# CASE STUDY: HOMESTEAD HIGH SCHOOL

## Written Spring 1998

Note how the examples in each of the three school snapshots demonstrate a commitment to active student participation in their learning and in the life of the school.

## A School Snapshot

At the beginning of the 1996–1997 school year, business owners located in the Homestead High School (HHS) vicinity complained to the Fremont Union High School District School Board about student littering and behavior during the lunch hour. HHS is an open campus, allowing students to leave the campus during the lunch break. At a board meeting in December attended by student leaders, the school board suggested that students attempt to solve this problem prior to the board taking any action regarding closing the campus.

Student leaders welcomed this opportunity to address an issue of importance to themselves and to the student body of the high school. To gather information and understand the issues that upset the merchants, students sponsored an open forum at a restaurant in the nearby shopping center. Invitations were delivered to students, parents, merchants, staff, community members, and law enforcement officials. Approximately one hundred people attended. Following the forum, student leaders identified five major problems: littering, lack of courtesy, drug use or sale, loitering, and smoking. The principal stated that drugs and smoking were administrative issues, but the other three should be addressed by the students.

Student leaders decided that the first step was to inform the student body of the problem. They knew that the vast majority of the students behaved in an acceptable manner during lunch, and that the behavior of a small minority of students might lead to loss of the open campus, a beloved privilege. A series of four student-led rallies were held to discuss the existing problem with students. A student who was respected by the students responsible for the problem volunteered to be one of the presenters. Law enforcement officials were also asked to explain the problem and the calls they received. The rallies were well received by students.

Next, student leaders, with principal support, closed the campus for two weeks. The purpose of this was to twofold: to demonstrate to students that a closed campus was a real possibility and to allow local businesses to feel the financial losses that would come with a closed campus. Within two days, local businesses called the school to voice support for continuing the open campus policy.

Third, students developed a system to monitor off-campus behavior on an ongoing basis. A flag system was instituted whereby student behavior was "graded" by fellow students, parents, and an administrator on a weekly basis. Consequences were clear. Since this system was instituted, the campus has been closed several times, but overall the behavior of students in nearby shopping centers has improved markedly.

The manner in which the school board and principal engaged students in determining and initiating solutions to a student-created problem clearly demonstrates a commitment to actively engage students in meaningful learning. Students were challenged to use their minds well, and they responded enthusiastically.

## School Background Information

HHS is one of five high schools in Fremont Union High School District. The school is located in Cupertino, California, in the heart of Silicon Valley. The enrollment is approximately 1,800 students, 54 percent white, not Hispanic, 10 percent Hispanic, 29 percent Asian, 7 percent other, with 9.3 percent English language learning students. It is a member of the Coalition of Essential Schools and was one of the first schools to receive funding and recognition as a lead school through the Bay Area School Reform Collaborative (Hewlett-Annenberg school reform initiative).

Study of school change began in September 1990 with common readings, speakers, and school visitations. Over the next two years, an increasing number of teachers exhibited enthusiasm for systemic school change. A redesign framework was written with broad input from staff, students, and parents. Interdisciplinary programs were begun that featured team teaching, project-based learning, and students exhibiting what they had learned. By 1998, approximately 40 percent of the students were involved in such programs sometime during their four years at HHS. At the same time, some teachers resisted. These teachers recruited parent and school board support for maintenance of the traditional program. Influential teachers and parents lined up on both sides of the debate. The local paper ran a series of articles about HHS's restructuring efforts. Throughout this time, the principal was clear with all parties that (1) he strongly supported and believed in the school restructuring initiative, and (2) student and parent voice should determine what percentage of the school program stayed traditional and what percentage would be designed around the initiative.

## A Second Snapshot

The 1997–1998 school year was spent "revisioning." The Coordinating Council, composed of teachers, classified staff, parents, and students, organized several initiatives to collect data from a wide range of constituencies to provide a basis for updating the school vision and the redesign framework. As a demonstration of commitment to student participation, fifteen students were trained as facilitators and led a series of student forums. Over a two-day period, teams of student facilitators met with two hundred students, randomly selected across grade levels, in groups of fifteen to twenty. Students were asked three questions about how they would like HHS to be in the future: What would students be doing? What would teachers be doing? How would parents and the broader community be involved? Student responses were then reviewed and summarized by the student facilitators and other students in the leadership class. Parents and staff were also surveyed and interviewed, using the same three questions. All results were presented to a task force of staff, students, and parents that developed recommendations and submitted them to the Coordinating Council.

I spent an hour with three of the student facilitators shortly after their meetings had concluded. They showed great pride for how much the school valued student voice, and in their role in helping this to occur. They talked about the importance given to student voice by the Coordinating Council, the School Site Council, the PTSA, and on various school task forces. They told me that during the previous year, when teachers at HHS had supported a work-to-rule order from the teacher's union, students formed a committee to learn about the reasons and the implications for student learning; they told me how respectful teachers were of this student effort. I also sat through much of the Coordinating Council meeting that same day. It was clear that the voices of the four student members were valued.

## Uniqueness of the School

*Clarity of Focus*

The redesign framework states: Our goal is to improve student learning by building better connections including

- connections among ideas, curricular areas, and student experiences;
- connections among people in the Homestead community, including students, staff, parents, and businesspeople;
- connections with the resources and opportunities in the world beyond the school.

In addition, the teachers working with the restructuring initiative are firmly committed to the principles of the Coalition of Essential Schools.

*Integrated Studies Programs*

Ninth- and tenth-grade students can choose to enroll in a foundation integrated studies program that involves instruction in English, social studies, math, science, art, and physical education. Approximately 25 percent choose this option each year. At the eleventh- and twelfth-grade level, students can choose to enroll in one of four integrated studies programs: media academy; science, technology and society; American studies; or advanced placement physics and calculus.

*Transitions: An Alternate Transcript for College Admissions*

Homestead, along with four other California high schools, is collaborating with the University of California and California State University admissions offices in developing and piloting an alternative school transcript to use in reviewing student applications. The transcript is based on curriculum and skills standards and an assessment rubric focused on "habits of mind," "knowledge," "communication skills," and "habits of work" rather than one letter grade for a class. These standards and the assessment rubric are used within the integrated studies programs at HHS, and, during spring 1998, were endorsed by the full faculty of the school.

*Restaurant*

HHS has a program to build the skills of tenth graders who failed half or more of their classes during ninth grade. As one of their projects, these students operate an on-campus restaurant for staff and students. The restaurant is managed by Chili's Restaurant, which trains the students in the skills, attitudes, and behaviors required to be effective workers in a restaurant setting.

*Service Learning*

All students enrolled in any of the eleventh- and twelfth-grade integrated studies programs are required to participate in formalized service learning and/or internship.

*School Governance*

Students participate in a wide variety of schoolwide governance activities. In addition to the ones just mentioned, students serve on the Administrative Leadership Team, meeting weekly with the principal, assistant principals, teacher association representative, and classified association representative.

## Student Outcomes—A Third Snapshot

*Student-Led Conferences*

> *As a result of the conferences, students have a sense of ownership over their work and learning. Students are better able to articulate what is expected of them. They talk articulately and sometimes eloquently about their work. This is something they've never been asked to do before.*
>
> —Lauri Steel, teacher

In 1997–1998, all students enrolled in the ninth- and tenth-grade integrated studies program prepared a portfolio of their work in the four areas listed previously under the Transitions Project: "habits of mind," "knowledge," "communication skills," and "habits of work." They wrote essays regarding their strengths and areas for growth for each of the four areas and in November and December presented their work to their parents and teachers at a conference facilitated by the student. This is a powerful example of student voice in curriculum and instruction at HHS.

I watched the video that was made of the conferences. It consists of one simulated conference viewed by all students in preparation for leading the conferences and two actual conferences. I was particularly impressed when one student said to her mother and teacher, "There are some things I need to work on. I need to learn to work in groups better. Second, I need to accept critiques from my peers better. Third, I need to work on my communication skills."

### Attendance

Students enrolled in the ninth- and tenth-grade integrated studies programs attend school more regularly than students enrolled in the traditional program. This is true for overall attendance and is particularly true for the percentage of students with five or more absences—12 percent integrated studies versus 20 percent traditional at grade nine and 10 percent integrated studies versus 16 percent traditional for Grade ten.

### Referrals for Inappropriate Behavior

At the ninth grade, there were far fewer behavioral referrals for students enrolled in the integrated studies program than for students enrolled in the traditional program—75 percent of ninth-grade students enrolled in the integrated studies program had no referrals compared to fewer than 50 percent of traditional students with no referrals.

### Teacher Comments

> I teach the Advanced Placement English class like a college class. Students who have come through the integrated studies programs are more willing to seek answers; the traditional students have trouble doing this. Their study skills and writing skills are about the same. The traditional

*students are better at tearing things apart; they classify very well. But the integrated studies students are better at seeing the broader picture.*

—Debbie Padilla, AP English teacher

*Integrated studies students are more comfortable with themselves. They are more outspoken and quicker to ask for help and to say when they don't understand something. They are more likely to see interdisciplinary connections. This is great for Socratic Seminars. For me as a teacher, I find these students very comfortable to be with and easier to form an honest relationship with.*

—Daniella Duran
Science, Technology, and Society, teacher

## A Final Word

It may be an oxymoron that any large comprehensive high school can be a resilient learning community. Many members of the HHS community are fighting the good fight. In the spring of 1998, David Payne, the principal since 1991, left to pursue other professional interests. At the time of this writing, it is unclear whether the initiatives begun will continue with the same passionate support from the new administration.

*Update Written Winter 2006–2007*

In 1998 HHS imploded. The principal and assistant principal for instruction left. The integrated studies programs for ninth and tenth grades and the work on alternative transcripts for college admission ceased. Service learning was no longer required. Student-led conferences ceased. Formal student roles in school governance were no longer stressed. Hostility among teachers ran strong. The new administrative team worked to unify the school community. Within a short time, many of the teachers engaged in the school change efforts also left. HHS is no longer a member of the Coalition of Essential Schools.

When I returned in spring and fall 2006, I expected that the school culture would still be toxic. I knew that Graham Clark was the third principal since 1998; three principals in eight years can be unsettling to a faculty, particularly at a school that had experienced the divisiveness that HHS had gone through.

How did this school earn a National Blue Ribbon of Excellent award in 2004?

In talking at length with the principal, teachers, and students, I found that the school had clearly healed. I wanted to understand how and why. I was given three reasons.

*The Urban High School Leadership Program (UHSLP)*

In 1998 the Educational Leadership Department at SJSU, my department, began offering a two-year master's program for high school teacher-leaders that also led to an administrative credential for graduates. This program was developed and coordinated by Dr. Marsha Speck. Enrollment was by school teams. The purpose was to prepare high school leaders to be assistant principals in urban high schools, with a focus on collaborative leadership and the importance of school leaders being skillful at staying focused on issues of equity and closing the achievement gap among its students. HHS had enrolled a team of four teachers in the initial cohort.

By 2006 five of the six administrators and fifteen HHS teachers had completed or were enrolled in UHSLP. All twenty of these people were very clear that this program had had a tremendous impact on their ability to lead and, as a result, a large impact on the workings and culture of the school. Graham talked about how UHSLP "is our leadership program." When I asked teachers what specific learnings from the program they had brought back to the school, they talked about use of data, a clear philosophy about the purpose of school, and the role of various forms of leadership, the importance of building relationships, and how they now used an equity lens in thinking through school issues. When I asked about the impact on how meetings were run, the teachers currently enrolled in UHSLP laughed and said that they were learning about that this week in class and that they had offered HHS practices as a positive model. The others talked about how, because of the learning in the program, good meeting practices were systemic in the school—organized agendas always out ahead of time, meeting norms developed and followed, various leadership roles rotated among participants, action plans, and notes that were circulated to all staff members.

*The Western Association of Schools and Colleges (WASC)*
*Report in 2000*

In California, in order to be accredited, all high schools do a self-study based on criteria and receive feedback from a visiting team every six years. When done well, this process can be very inclusive of the school community and used to seriously reflect on school strengths and areas of concern. It offers the opportunity to develop an action plan for school improvement focused on the needs of students. Teachers talked with me about how positive this process had been for helping with the healing process. Then principal Al Montgomery is well known for building consensus and fostering a strong school culture. Teachers talked in glowing terms about the positive impact of his leadership style. HHS is going through the next WASC review this year and an inclusive, student-focused process continues to be used. The teacher coordinating the report is a graduate of UHSLP.

*Block Scheduling*

Four years ago, HHS initiated block scheduling. Teachers and administrators shared with me that the collaborative process used to reach consensus on this change helped build the positive school culture that exists now. For the initial adoption of the block, 67 percent of the faculty voted for implementation. The collaborative process continued, with strong professional development support, and 80 percent approval was attained to continue for the second year.

Several governance structures have been put in place to foster a positive, inclusive culture. Teachers estimated that there are about fifty formal roles that teachers can be involved in that help lead the school and that at least one-third of the teachers are in such roles.

*The School Planning Team (SPT)*

SPT grew out of the previous WASC report. SPT meets twice a month, is open to any interested staff member, and has as its primary task the coordination of the professional development plan for the school. HHS has collaboration time every Monday morning, with students arriving late. Teachers choose one "resource group" to participate in for the year. Examples of resource groups are meeting the needs of English language learners, algebra, community partnerships, AVID Understanding by Design, and community building. These groups are teacher led. Teachers talked about all of the opportunities to be teacher-leaders and how they are trusted by administration to do these roles well. When the school was considering the move to block schedule, SPT coordinated the conversation.

### Staff Senate

Twelve teachers are elected to the senate, which serves as a forum for staff to raise issues. The principal attends and coordinates responses to issues as appropriate. Thus, other meetings are not diverted by issues teachers want discussed, and there is a clear forum for teachers to be heard and their issues addressed. The people I talked with said that the senate had been a vital communication tool when discussing block scheduling. I have seen numerous senates at other schools become negative influences on the school, but all comments at HHS were positive.

### Department Chairs

Department chairs meet once a month with the principal. The focus of this meeting is primarily on instructional management issues. The union contract has specific language about class size, teacher-student ratios, and percent of money for salary and for other purposes. Graham explained to me how important it is to inform everyone about how the master schedule is developed and much of this is done collaboratively with department chairs.

### District

The district meets with department chairs both as a district group and by academic discipline. Beginning in 2006 the deputy superintendent for instruction has led conversations focused on the role of department heads as school leaders. The district has prioritized algebra and meeting the needs of English language learners. This led to the inclusion of both as "resource groups" at HHS, and positive articulation has come as a result. On a less serious note, recently there was a districtwide teacher dodge-ball tournament that built camaraderie among teachers and was very well attended by students.

*Parents*

There is an active School Site Council and Parent-Student-Teacher Association (PTSA). Teachers, students, and parents are active in both. This is a community with many parents who are actively involved in their children's education and want a voice at the school.

The focus of the initial case study was on student voice. Whereas the voices of students are not as formally engaged as in the past, their voices are important. Three years ago, it was determined that tension existed among various student groups. Beginning in 2005–2006 and continued in 2006–2007 the school has held "challenge days," two in 2005–2006, and two in 2006–2007. Students are nominated to participate by teachers or by students. One hundred are chosen each time to spend a day together and with teachers breaking down the communication barriers that exist among students. The benefit of these days was talked about by teachers and students during my interviews with them. Also, resulting from a recognition that not all students were being successful, the school initiated an Advancement Via Individual Determination program (AVID, www.avidonline.org). Currently servicing student Grades nine to eleven (twelfth grade will be added next year). AVID focuses on creating a college-going culture for students with high potential but needing support with academic skills.

When meeting with the student council, I asked about student voice. They talked about challenge days, and they talked about how administration came to them earlier this year concerned about "dirty dancing" at school dances, asking the student council to come up with strategies to address the concerns. The student council talked about the concerns and decided to change the music at dances. As students talked with me about this issue, they seemed proud to have been asked and even prouder that they had worked to solve the problem. Students are represented at the PTSA and on the school board, and the current president of the school site council is a student.

## Conclusion

I asked teachers, "How in the world has this school, so deeply divided just a few years ago, healed so well?" They talked about learning the lessons from the past and consciously focusing on ways to build a strong culture. They talked about the importance of skillful collaboration and building relationships, trust, and communication. They talked about being at a school at which no one pointed fingers anymore because opportunities were there for everyone to lead and to be heard. And they talked about the importance of current administrators being role models, visible, open, and trusting. They asked me to include how the transition from Al Montgomery to Graham Clark as principals had been seamless because Graham spent the first months listening. They told me that when the first crisis hit, he earned the respect of the faculty by solving the issue by listening, acting firmly, and not blaming. Finally, they told me that because they are treated as professionals and their voices truly valued, the respect among faculty and among faculty and support staff is very strong and collaborative.

### Homestead High School
21370 Homestead RD
Cupertino, CA 95014
408-522-2500
Web site: www. hhs.fushd.org

| **Enrollment:** | **2,089** |
| --- | --- |
| African American | 3% |
| Asian | 33% |
| Filipino | 2% |
| Hispanic | 11% |
| White (not Hispanic) | 51% |

| API | 1999* | 2005 | 2006 | Change |
| --- | --- | --- | --- | --- |
| Total | 749 | 824 | 842 | +93 |
| Hispanic | NA | 643 | 666 | +23 |
| White (not Hispanic) | 778 | 840 | 880 | +102 |
| Asian | 776 | 871 | 885 | +109 |

* not enough students in this category to be numerically significant

CHAPTER SEVEN

# Managing Change

*On Your Mark, Get Set,*
*Are You Ready to Go?*

*One of the central lessons we think we have learned about*
*previous rounds of innovation is that they failed because*
*they didn't get at fundamental, underlying, systemic features*
*of school life: they didn't change the behaviors, norms, and*
*beliefs of practitioners. Consequently, these reforms ended*
*up being grafted on to existing practices, and they were*
*greatly modified, if not fully overcome, by those practices.*

—Evans, 1996, p. 5

I wish that I could write this chapter as a step-by-step, easy-to-
follow list of how to change your school into a resilient learning
community. Unfortunately, the history of school and personal
change clearly tells us that such rationalistic approaches ignore
what it means to lead and manage change. People are far too irra-
tional and far too comfortable with the status quo for an easy-to-
follow list approach to have any positive, lasting impact on people's

behaviors, norms, and beliefs. For a school to become a resilient learning community, the depth of change required in the culture of the school—in its deeply held beliefs—requires a concerted effort and commitment too deep to be addressed by a one-way-fits-all approach. It has taken me over fifty years to reach the vision I have for public schooling. I cannot expect others to be at the same place. I must honor their journey, and I must be prepared for their questions and resistance.

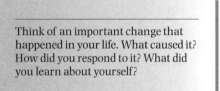

Think of an important change that happened in your life. What caused it? How did you respond to it? What did you learn about yourself?

## WHAT WE DO KNOW ABOUT CHANGE

- *Change* is external and situational. Transition is the psychological process every person goes through in order to adjust to change and is therefore internal. Therefore, leading and managing change and transition means working with individuals, often one person at a time, to help each person acknowledge the need for change, accept the end to the old, and begin to internalize the behaviors, norms, and beliefs that go with the new. This is particularly hard work since almost everyone would rather defend the old rather than seriously consider the new. It takes far more time than most of us recognize and are willing to give. We will continue to muddle through a range of failed school reform efforts unless we take the time and develop the skills, attitudes, and behaviors to do it right. Managing and leading change and transition requires skillful leadership and can be learned.

Managing and leading change and transition requires above all that leaders be skillful at fostering resilience. When people know that you care about them, that you have high expectations for them and will support them, and that you value their participation, it is far more likely that they will accept change and make the necessary transitions. Please, reread this paragraph since it is so central to what this book is about.

The reader is encouraged to read William Bridges's (1991) book *Managing Transitions: Making the Most of Change* and Robert Evans's (1996) book *The Human Side of School Change.* These two books significantly influenced the content of this chapter.

- Change starts with ourselves. The only person we can change is oneself. This is why we need to clarify our own vision and acknowledge that a vision is ever evolving. We need to work on our own behaviors, norms, and beliefs. We need to actively practice good listening skills. We need to be courageous. We need to be sure that we—you and I—truly believe in the ability of all students, regardless of race, ethnicity, gender, language, and socioeconomic status, to learn the habits of mind needed to use their minds and hearts well.

- School culture is largely determined by career teachers and staff. Many successful corporations were founded by individuals who established a corporate culture that became the company way and spent their careers building their corporations around that culture. Schools are different! School and district administrators, students, and parents come and go. The career teachers and classified staff are the constants who establish the unwritten rules for the way the school does its business. Therefore, school change involves transitions for people who have dedicated their lives to doing things a certain way. They know from experience that if they passively resist the changes desired, the change agent will probably stop pushing and/or leave. They also know that if they actively engage in the change efforts, the change agent will still leave, and a new change agent with a different agenda will soon be on the scene.

For most school employees, their experience with school change is negative and deeply emotional. Either they feel defensive, or their past efforts at reform were not successful. In either case, they are not hopeful.

Building relationships and working collaboratively with career teachers and with classified staff are among the most important skills leaders must learn and practice. I have taught new school administrators since 1991. One of the first issues they confront is how to work successfully with an experienced secretary or custodian.

- Anyone and everyone can be a leader. Strong leadership and student learning are closely linked. Often leadership is identified with a principal or superintendent. However, in reality, important leadership comes from teachers and often from classified staff, and also from key parents and students. As a principal, I knew that key teacher-leaders, the secretary, the custodian, and several parents had at least as much influence within the school community as I did. When we worked together, good things happened. If we did not, few people followed. Enlisting, empowering, and trusting others to lead effectively is an important skill that good leaders have mastered. Read Krovetz and Arriaza (2006).

## WHAT WE CAN DO WITH WHAT WE KNOW

### Start With Yourself

Your deeply held beliefs are at the heart of who you are as an educational leader. If you believe that all students are capable of developing the habits of mind to use their minds and hearts well, you are ready to place this at the center of your vision. If you believe that the protective factors of resilience influence students' ability to learn, you are ready to advocate for resilient learning communities. If, when people are talking with you, you are present to their ideas and concerns, you are a good listener. If you are trustworthy, you will have people willing to follow you. If you believe that everyone can be a leader, you are ready to lead. The reader is encouraged to spend time collecting data and honesty answering the questions in Figure 7.1.

*Essential Conversations*

Helping people accept that change is necessary begins with the conversations that we have with colleagues about our deeply held beliefs and our vision for how these beliefs should be implemented. I find that many school leaders have not shared their beliefs or their vision with their colleagues. Many teachers cannot tell you that what their principal feels is really important. Many teachers do not know what is important to the teacher in the next room. If we believe that all students are capable of using their minds and hearts well, then we need to believe the same for the adults in the school. Essential conversations are about challenging adults to use their minds and hearts well and to develop and use the habits of mind we want all students to develop.

---

**Figure 7.1**     Self-Assess Your Behaviors, Norms, and Beliefs

1. Think about your conversations with the three students. Do you really believe each is capable of learning to use his or her mind and heart well? Where are they being successful? Why? Where are they not successful? Why not? What is blocking their learning? What would it take to overcome this? Look deeply at your answers and your attitudes.

2. Think about the three protective factors for resilience. In what ways are these powerful factors in your life? How do they affect each of the three students?

3. Assess your listening skills. Ask others to give you honest feedback regarding how they know if you are an active listener. How do you know if others are actively listening to you? Practice, practice, practice.

4. How do you know if people trust you? You may want insight and feedback from a good friend or from a professional counselor. Put aside your defenses and seek honest feedback. What objective evidence do you have?

5. How do you view leadership? If you believe in shared leadership, how do you demonstrate this belief? What evidence can you offer? Please read Lambert (2003), Katzenmeyer and Moller (2001), and Krovetz and Arriaza (2006).

6. There is really only one way for you to accurately self-assess. Look yourself in the mirror and think about the three students. What would each of them say about their relationship with you? Is it based on caring? Do you have high expectations for them and support them? Do you value their participation? What evidence would they put forth about you? If you have the courage, ask for their feedback.

---

Essential conversations require that leaders be reflective thinkers, active listeners, and courageous. Innovation will always encounter major resistance if implementation is defined according to only one reality, that of "the leader." Essential conversations occur when we discuss ideas and feelings that are important to us, and we truly listen to the other person. We must be open to the idea that our vision is not more correct than anyone else's vision.

We must be sincerely open to questioning our vision and allowing it to evolve. Being open to sharing our beliefs, hopes, and desires with others, knowing that they may not be popular, requires that one open up oneself to one's colleagues. Very often people will disagree vehemently with you. You need to be able to separate the intellectual discourse of your ideas from attacks on you as a person. Do not take the disagreement personally; it is seldom meant that way. In case it does get personal, stop the conversation and refocus on the ideas, not the people. This requires courage.

Essential conversations involve the exchange of ideas and the pursuit of shared goals, which, in my opinion, requires that leaders be readers. When I walk into the office of a principal or superintendent and see only manuals on the bookshelves—no books and journals—I assume that this person is not a reader and therefore probably not a thoughtful leader. This is a stereotype I know, but nonetheless one I hold dear. In the very busy and stressful life that is being a school leader, you must find time to read, reflect, and converse. Reading and reflection help us form our vision. Essential conversations are required to rethink and refine our beliefs and vision, to challenge others to do the same, and to help people start to reach consensus. Being a part of essential conversations should be one of the joyful parts of the job.

In my classes for aspiring and beginning school administrators and teacher leaders, I always begin class by asking, "What's become clear since last we met?" a Ralph Waldo Emerson quote that is meant to say that I am really interested in their reflections. I tell them that self-reflection is not enough. If they are to be effective leaders, they must talk with people they work with. I expect and require them to take the ideas, discussions, and readings from class to their colleagues.

*Readings to Start Wtih*

- Bonnie Benard, Debbie Meier, Ted Sizer, Roland Barth, Linda Lambert, Linda Darling-Hammond, Glenn Singleton, Marty Krovetz
- *Educational Leadership*, the Association for Supervision and Curriculum Development (ASCD; www.ascd.org) monthly journal

- *Horace*, a publication of the Coalition of Essential Schools (www.essentialschools.org)
- Anything a colleague gives you to read

## Support Your Own Reflection

- Set aside at least two hours per week for professional reading. Use this time religiously.
- Maintain a journal.
- Use a tape recorder when you drive to record thoughts.
- Join ASCD and other professional organizations. Take advantage of their resources and conferences.
- Organize a regular meeting of interested peers, within and outside your school, to reflect together. My breakfasts are quite well known in Santa Cruz.

*Practices That Support Essential Conversations*

- Any time teachers come to together, the focus should be on collaboration and sharing, not on information giving. Change all meetings, especially staff meetings, to reflect this.
- Circulate articles and parts of books to colleagues. Follow up with informal conversations. Keep after people so that they will expect you to talk with them about readings and ideas. Read and initiate conversation any time someone gives you something to read. Be an active listener. Be patient; it will take some people time to get involved in these conversations.
- Using the three students you have focused on, start positive conversations with other adults who know these students.
- Be courageous! Let people know that you will not participate in negative talk about students, parents, teachers, and administrators.
- Welcome opportunities to participate in conversations that focus on positive problem solving.

## Assess How Well Your School Community Fosters Resilience

Collect data regularly and purposefully and use those data to inform and guide decision making. Collect data based on well-conceived questions. There is little reason to collect data if it is not being done with a clear purpose.

When collecting data, it is important that you look at a wide variety of school data. Always collect at least three different types of data to answer any question; this is called *triangulation*. As a leadership team, plan ways to collect data that will be meaningful to the staff and community. Engage the whole staff, parents, and students in collaborative action research—in defining the problem, defining the data to collect, collecting the data, analyzing the data, developing action plans in response to the data, and evaluating the effectiveness of the results of the action plan. Excellent resources include Richard Sagor's (1993) book *How to Conduct Collaborative Action Research* and Web sites dedicated to action research (www.alliance.brown.edu/dnd/ar_websites.shtml). See Figure 7.2.

---

**Figure 7.2**   Format for Defining an Action Research Project

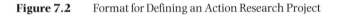

**BACKGROUND** (What is the prevailing practice? What is the history of this practice? What does data indicate is the impact of this practice?)

**PROBLEM STATEMENT**
The problem is that

**PURPOSE STATEMENT**
The purpose is to

**RESEARCH QUESTIONS**
1.

2.

3.

**DATA REQUIRED**

**SIGNIFICANCE OF THIS PROJECT**

**EVALUATION: HOW WILL YOU KNOW IF YOU ARE MORE EFFECTIVE?**

---

Use one or more of the instruments discussed in Figure 7.3 and included to assess how well your school fosters resilience for your students. Gather data from a large segment of your school community. Collect this data in a variety of ways—focus groups, individual interviews, surveys, and direct observation.

---

**Figure 7.3**    Assessing How Well Your School Fosters Resilience

---

- **Resource A in this book**
  Use the tools in this book to guide walkthroughs of your school. Do this alone. Do it with peers. Do it with students and parents.
- **Assessing School Resiliency Building** developed by Nan Henderson and included in Henderson and Milstein (1996) (Resource B)
  I have used this instrument along with Bonnie Benard's 1991 article with numerous school leadership teams and with my students at San Jose State University to help them reflect on resilience as the foundation of their own deeply held beliefs about student learning, to assess the current conditions at their school, and to develop an action plan to make the school a more resilient community for the students and adults.
- **Moving from Risk to Resiliency in Our Schools: Creating Opportunities to Learn** developed by Bonnie Benard (Resource C)
  This rubric is very easy to use and a simple way to involve people in a meaningful discussion about resilience and the current conditions at their school.
- **Self-Reflection Resilience Checklist** developed by Bonnie Benard (Resource D)
  This is a simple checklist that school personnel can use to assess their commitment to the three protective factors.
- **WestEd Resilience, Youth Development and Asset Assessment tools, including the Health Kids Survey** (Flyers in Resource E)

In Chapters 4, 5, and 6, I offer a list of school practices that you could expect to see at a school committed to being a resilient learning community. Assess which of these are in place and effective at your school. Collect this data in a variety of ways—focus groups, individual interviews, surveys, direct observation (see Resource A for a compilation of these lists).

Look at student work for evidence. Base data collection on the following two questions: (1) What is it that we want all students to understand, know and be able to do? (2) How are we going to know if students understand, know, and can do these things? Student work should always be a primary data source. Utilize standardized test data as one of the important data sources; your community has high expectations for how your students will perform on these tests. However, make sure that other examples of student work are tied closely to students exhibiting the use of their minds and hearts. Student work should be reviewed by teams of teachers, based on clear standards and focused on question 1. The Coalition of Essential Schools has proposed a procedure called Tuning Protocol, which is a very useful way for teachers to do such a review of student work (Cushman, 1995).

Always look at student data by subgroup, such as race, ethnicity, gender, grade, length of time enrolled at your school, English speaker/English language learner. This is called *disaggregation*.

*Develop an Action Plan*

Use assessment data with staff, parents, and students to reach consensus on a plan that will clearly focus on fostering resilience for all students and adults in your school community. Do not wait until everyone buys into the vision; that will never occur, and the vision will continue to evolve over time anyway. Figure 7.4 details the necessary components of an action plan.

---

**Figure 7.4**    Components of an Action Plan

The action plan should include

- a clear belief statement focused on the protective factors of resilience;
- the givens—agreements of what is important and nonnegotiable; this could be written as a compact that participants sign, indicating agreement and commitment;
- a limited number of important goal statements (three or four) that deal directly with the protective factors for students and adults;
- a limited number of objectives and activities (two or three) related to each goal;
- clear ways that people will measure progress, long term and particularly short term, for each objective and activity; remember to triangulate and disaggregate data;
- ways to learn and celebrate as each objective and activity is completed—learn and celebrate often;
- clear agreement on how the effectiveness of the action plan will be documented;
- timeline and people responsible for leadership at each step;
- communication procedures for each step;
- timeline for revisiting, revisioning, and revising the action plan.

*Evaluate the Effectiveness of What You Do*

Be honest! Collect meaningful data and share the data in order to make informed decisions about the effectiveness of your efforts. Data should be driven by the questions used to generate your action plan. Data should be at least triangulated, so that a variety of different types of data is collected, and disaggregated, so that you can be specific with recommendations that result from using the data to make decisions. This can be time-consuming. It can be risky if results do not support your goals, and at times, data will not appear to support your goals.

Too often, schools do not collect meaningful data, and therefore cannot demonstrate the effectiveness of good work to their various publics. Too often, we do not explain data collected in a way that the public can understand and value. In addition, we are unable to adjust our work because we don't have the accurate information needed to make purposeful decisions. Our redesign efforts will not be sustained over time if we do not make good decisions based on sound data.

*Understand the Importance of Transitions and Endings*

Every change in an organization leads to some sort of change in the lives of the people in that organization. People lose turf, attachments, sense of future, meaning, and control. It is natural for people to wonder why there is a need for change unless what they are currently doing is inadequate, and therefore people feel criticized personally by a call for change. The more we, as leaders, understand what will change and for whom, the better we are prepared to help people with their transitions and therefore to

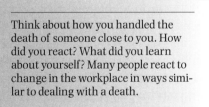

Think about how you handled the death of someone close to you. How did you react? What did you learn about yourself? Many people react to change in the workplace in ways similar to dealing with a death.

accept endings. Leadership and management of change requires that we anticipate the grieving and overreaction that comes with transitions, that we acknowledge the losses openly and sympathetically, that we communicate over and over in a wide variety of ways, that we treat the past with respect, and that we show how the endings ensure the continuity of what really matters from the past. All of this is explained very well by Bridges (1991, Chapter 3).

Often we think that mandating a change is enough, or explaining it is enough. Then we wonder why what we wanted was not implemented enthusiastically and sustained over time. In fact, people need to acknowledge that endings have occurred and transition to the new way of doing things. This requires changes in behaviors, norms, and beliefs. Skillful, well-planned, broad-based leadership can facilitate this process. As Evans (1996) writes, "Many educational change efforts fail due to expectable problems that well-trained leaders would anticipate" (p. 4).

When I coach school leadership teams, I work with them to try to predict what every staff member would lose if the proposed changes were to occur and how each staff member is likely to behave. Then, each member of the leadership team (typically several teachers, the principal, and sometimes classified staff) selects two or three staff members whom he or she will support through the transition process. We revisit this support effort on a regular basis. This is not manipulative and dishonest. It is important leadership in the management and leadership of change and transition.

A number of years ago, an experienced principal I know was transferred to a different school in her district. The new school had had a series of unsuccessful principals, and she was expected to refocus the school in positive ways. She was known and respected by many of the teachers at this school. At the end of the first year, she felt that she was being successful, but also felt that some teachers were not happy with her leadership. She asked me to spend time walking around the campus talking with people, and to share with her my sense of the school climate. I spent time on the school campus and told her that it seemed her leadership had led to several teachers losing their turf. When teachers were unhappy with previous principals, they congregated in the parking lot after school to complain to each other. Now that the school was headed in a more positive direction, the leaders of those complaining had no audience. The lesson is no matter how positive and desired the change, losses occur that make the transitions difficult for some people.

*Sell the Problem, Not the Solution*

Meaningful change will not be implemented unless people are persuaded that there is a problem and they are involved in helping find the solution. People must be made uncomfortable with the status quo and their role in maintaining it. This should be done while helping people feel competent and hopeful to improve the situation. If teachers are made to feel incompetent, a natural reaction to being told that what they are currently doing is not working, they will resist and blame others—the students, parents, and administration—for the identified problems.

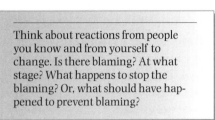

Think about reactions from people you know and from yourself to change. Is there blaming? At what stage? What happens to stop the blaming? Or, what should have happened to prevent blaming?

At the same time, through essential conversations focused on students and their work, teachers and staff can be helped to accept that many of our current practices and many of our current beliefs and norms are counterproductive. Only by collaboratively accepting responsibility as a school community—teachers, staff, administrators, parents, students, and community—for the success of all students will we truly be proud of the quality of student work.

Using student work as the focus of collaborative study encourages us to see the problem firsthand. Examine data from at least three sources (triangulation) and look at the data for specific subgroups (disaggregation).

Teachers and administrators at Mission Hill Junior High School (MHJHS) spent much of the 1990–1992 school years looking at and talking about school practices and student work, reading, and visiting other schools. Survey data was gathered from students and parents. At an all-day planning session, teachers drafted a statement describing how they would like the school to be. They then graded the school against their ideal. Overall, they gave themselves a grade of D. The time taken to reflect collaboratively on the ideal versus current practices, and careful facilitation by the school leadership team, led the staff to agree to major redesign. The case study at the end of this chapter is about this journey. An important part of this journey is the major leadership roles played by key teachers and classified staff.

### Clarity and Focus

Very often, when I am talking with a school principal, she will tell me about her vision for the school and express frustration with how few teachers have bought into it. My first question is, "If I were to ask teachers what your vision is, what would they tell me?" All too often, the principal responds, "I'm really not sure they know. I want to be collaborative and let them develop the school vision." Wrong answer! How can people trust you if they don't know what you stand for? The idea is not to impose your vision, but to make it an integral part of the discussion. If you want students and adults to use their minds and hearts well, you need to model this behavior publicly and often.

Teachers often see and hear a leader's vision as a series of unrelated and unimportant changes for the sake of change. Three characteristics of effective leadership are (1) the ability to create a picture of the whole that others can see, (2) consistency of support for efforts leading toward fulfillment of this whole, and (3) the willingness to protect people from other changes that are irrelevant to the effort.

At the same time, one's vision is ever evolving. On many occasions, often when I thought my vision was clearest, someone would ask me a question that either I could not answer or that gave me new insight. Being an active listener and a collaborative problem solver allows the vision leaders bring to the school to evolve into a shared vision of the school community.

*Courageous Leadership and Courageous Followership*

I have used the word *courageous* several times in this book. Taking risks with your peers, with those you supervise, and with those who supervise you takes courage. Prioritizing your time, when you are already working sixty-plus hours per week, to read, start essential conversations, and make fostering resilience the passionate focus of school life takes courage. Be courageous! Ira Chaleff (1995) has written an excellent book about courage and leadership titled *The Courageous Follower: Standing Up To and For Our Leaders.*

## THE SECTION YOU'VE ALL BEEN WAITING FOR: WHAT ABOUT ALL THE RESISTANCE?

In my experience, there are primarily two types of resisters to change. The first are usually very vocal and often very political. They disagree with you because their deeply held beliefs are passionately held, and your vision does not seem to be compatible with their beliefs. These people are often very talented teachers who work long hours and are highly valued by students and parents. Many high school principals will talk about their math teachers as being highly dedicated teachers who always get in the way of change. Too often, we define these people as the enemy, when we should be nurturing them. Michael Fullan (1998) writes about respecting those you want to silence. They are the conscience of the school! If I cannot answer their questions to my satisfaction (probably not to their satisfaction), I am not ready to answer the questions from people interested in our redesign efforts. I learn from their questions; I need to hear their discontent; I need to not judge them because of their views, but to accept their views as valid views of their world, a world that overlaps with mine. As a principal, I spent at least as much time talking one on one and in small groups with these individuals as with people in favor of the redesign efforts. When they got personal, I learned to stop them and to tell them that was not okay, that I was every bit as dedicated as they and demanded the same respect from them that they wanted from me. I valued their input, valued them as teachers, and valued them as people. When I think about the teachers I miss most from my days as principal, it is these dedicated teachers whom I think of.

The second group can be characterized as passive-aggressive teachers who do not want to change because they have become comfortable with the compromises they have made and no longer have high expectations for themselves. Because they are less verbal, it can be harder to engage them and to know what they honestly believe. They may say they agree with the definition of the problem and even with the solutions, but they put little energy into fostering resilience and into their teaching lives. They may be a large percentage of your teaching staff. These people were much harder for me to work with than the first group. To be successful as a leader of change and transition, you need to recognize that many of these people will transition if they see other teachers they respect doing the same first, and if you are consistent with them in terms of fostering resilience for them. Therefore, the member of the leadership team who agrees to work with one of these people should be respected by that person. In addition, it is important that you be clear about your high expectations and purposeful support for them. In some cases, this will have to be documented in formal evaluations. Some of these teachers will need to leave the school and perhaps the profession. Courageous leadership is critically important with this group.

## A FINAL WORD

The primary purpose of this book is to help school leaders understand and apply the principles of resilience as a guide for proactive, systemic school redesign. My experience in sharing resilience with others is that it makes sense to people. Sharing how a resilient learning community must stress the protective factors for the adults as well as for the students is very engaging to teachers. Teachers and administrators know the many ways their school does not offer this. They are eager to share the ideas with colleagues and to devote time and resources to improve the situation. I do not mean to intimate that change then becomes easy. The key underlying belief in the potential of all students is not widely supported in belief or practice. The norms and behaviors that must change to truly become a resilient learning community are deeply embedded in school practice. However, most people would like to be part of a resilient learning community and certainly want their children to attend such a school.

Several years ago, I asked a group of high school teachers and administrators to share with each other what they would show their own child at their school if their child was an eighth grader and they wanted their child to attend their high school. I had been working with this group of twenty-five teachers and principals for several months. We were focusing on the protective factors of resilience as the core of their school action plan, and commitment to follow through with peers at their schools was coming slowly. Suddenly, one teacher looked at a second teacher, who was a recognized leader within our group, and said, "You do have an eighth-grade daughter. Where will she go to high school next year?" The answer was a private high school. The room became silent. Every person in that room was ashamed, for all knew that they might make the same choice. No longer was this an intellectual exercise. People got serious about developing action plans, using resilience as the focus, that they could proudly take back to their schools to facilitate discussion and action.

# CASE STUDY: MISSION HILL MIDDLE SCHOOL

## Written Spring 1998

This case study is longer than the previous ones. It is important that the reader see the intricacies and stressors of the change process. You should be able to see how each of the points raised in this chapter relates to the experiences at Mission Hill Middle School. In 1998 the school was a junor high school. When sixth grade was added later it became Mission Hill Middle School. So, in this section junior high school is appropriate.

## Introduction

Restructuring a school is like undertaking a major remodeling of a house. When a family has lived fairly comfortably in a house for a long time, the need for change presents itself gradually over time. The member(s) most affected by the inadequacies of the current living conditions begins to talk about change. He or she shares this vision for change with others living in the same house, hoping that the other person (people) will instantly see the same need for change that the first person has taken years to visualize clearly. Plans are drawn. Preparation for the remodeling occurs. Work begins. Everyone must give up the comfort of the old patterns. Unexpected complications cannot be predicted. Stress increases. Relationships are challenged. Interim changes have to be made that may compromise the vision.

## Realizing the Need for Change

What had begun as individual personal and professional growth journeys for many staff members led key staff leaders to the consensus that there was a need for a new strategic plan that focused on powerful learning for all students. They realized that the existing methods of schooling were grossly inadequate.

MHJHS was a heavily tracked, departmentalized junior high school and a Distinguished California School. The school's growing

population of limited-English-speaking students and special education students was segregated from the mainstream students. In
spring 1991 the school district hired a new principal, the eighth
principal in twelve years.

## Sharing the Need for Change

Who says it's broken? We're a distinguished school.

Beginning in the spring of 1991, staff leaders carefully
orchestrated a carefully planned effort to gain acceptance for the
need to change MHJHS. The bullets that follow highlight activities
of the next twelve months.

- The leadership team applied unsuccessfully for a California
  school restructuring planning grant. We didn't get it, but
  we were committed and vowed to keep going and to reapply.
- Seventeen staff members agreed to continue studying
  ways to change practice at MHJHS to meet the needs of all
  students.
- These teachers read, visited other schools, attended conferences together, and talked extensively among themselves.
- These teachers led a series of well-designed focus groups,
  looking at school performance issues with the entire staff.
- A planning team met weekly from four to seven o'clock from
  the end of January 1992 until the end of the school year
  planning, developing potential implementation models for
  the school, and talking about ways to help each staff member
  make the personal transitions necessary to allow for implementation of a new model for educating their students.

## Envisioning a Dream House

*A Pivotal Day*

On February 11, 1992, at an all-school planning day, information from a student survey regarding "what is" from students'
point of view was shared with staff. Students expressed feelings of
alienation from staff and from each other; they felt that the curriculum was disjointed. Thus, the focus of the day was to help staff
"get in touch with the disgruntled client." A new mission statement was drafted by staff that reflected beliefs about what is best

for kids and how the school must address these beliefs every day. Staff graded the school against their ideal and gave themselves a D. The question was asked if working harder would make a difference, or whether the school needed to change. A vote was taken, and over 95 percent of the staff voted to make significant changes over the next five years.

- On February 19 twenty-two of twenty-seven staff members attended a voluntary meeting to do short- and long-term planning as a follow-up to the previous week's meeting. Staff agreed that "connectedness" among teachers, students, parents, community, student support services, and subject areas needed to serve as the focus for all restructuring and remodeling efforts.
- On March 13 staff met all day. The staff agreed that certain things were to change. The school would be reorganized into teams and a student advisory system would be implemented. Special education, limited-English-speaking, and Title I students would be mainstreamed for all core classes. Detracking would occur in academic subjects. Numerous details still needed to be worked out. The leadership team was charged with the responsibility of developing more specific plans for staff input.

## Drawing the Blueprint—Gaining Building Permits

- On March 25 the leadership team took a new state restructuring grant proposal to the Santa Cruz City Schools School Board. All members of the board indicated overwhelming support and approval for the breadth of the proposed changes and the innovative aspects. In addition, the remodeling of two science labs was approved by a financially strapped district.

One board member capsulated the entire board's response by stating, "This is the most positive proposal I've had to vote on since I was elected to the board."

The plan that was unanimously approved included the following:

- Grade-level academic teams
- Two-hour academic core classes (humanities and/or math/ science)

- Student advisory program
- Heterogeneous grouping (inclusion)
- Thematic units that were integrated and interdisciplinary
- Project-based instruction
- Common preparation time for each of the four teams
- Conflict resolution program
- Seventh-period selective program

## Temporary Plans for the Remodel

In anticipation of restructuring for 1992–1993, staff preferences were surveyed. The plan was still in need of specifics. Teams had to be formed; rooms needed to be assigned; teacher assignments had to be set. It was important to plan for support and professional development. Some took advantage; some did not. The following questions were asked:

1. Who would you feel comfortable teaming with?

2. What support do you need?

3. What training do you want?

4. What do you want to teach?

5. What are you not willing to give up?

The principal negotiated with each teacher in order to try to give that teacher the support and encouragement necessary to feel prepared to implement the remodeling plans. At times, this meant that those who were most supportive of the remodel were accommodated less than those who were less supportive.

The bidding began—"Who'll take Mr. X? . . . Not me, I had him last time."

The faculty voted to proceed with implementation in the fall with or without the additional state funding. In August the funding was denied by the state.

## We Didn't Get This One Either

During summer 1992 a team of fifteen teachers received integrated thematic instruction training through the Bay Area Middle School Project (BAMS). Some members from each of the four new academic teams attended. Considerable team building occurred as a result of this collaborative experience. The coordinator of BAMS was hired to coach staff in implementing integrated thematic instruction and group dynamics. Also during the summer, the school district refurbished two science classrooms to facilitate hands-on science, and a group of teachers wrote materials for the new student advisory program. In addition, the principal and library-media specialist scheduled and solicited community volunteers for the student selective program; students would be offered a broad selective program during seventh period, with minicourses offered by teacher and community volunteers.

## Fall 1992—Work Begins (Torn Up and No End in Sight)

The plan that was created by the staff and enthusiastically supported by the board was not a one-room remodel. It was a "from-the-ground-up" renovation. Once in the middle of the renovation, many wished they had never begun. Daily life was harder. Cooperative planning took more time. Dealing with a broader range of students was challenging. Meetings increased tenfold. Stress increased. It was hard to maintain the enthusiasm for a potentially better school.

We knew we had a good plan. We felt that we were ready. We thought we knew exactly what we were doing. Unlike the unsinkable Titanic, we had provided lifeboats; however not everyone chose to use one.

## Observations: Anticipating and Experiencing Are Two Different Things

*Everyone Gave up Something*

Several teachers were teaching at new grade levels. The number of math tracks had been reduced from four to two. Science was now integrated and hands on. The variety of electives was limited, since elective teachers were needed to teach core classes. Special education and bilingual teachers were no longer teaching in self-contained programs. The Title I/bilingual coordinator was now working with the entire staff rather than with a limited number of teachers. Teachers were trying to broaden their teaching repertoires in order to meet the needs of heterogeneous classes of students.

*Unexpected Complications*

Lower than expected school enrollment led to a reduction in funds received from the district. Inadequate state funding led to a reduction in classified support staff and counselors districtwide. No state restructuring money made it even more difficult. Personal considerations prompted the assistant principal to leave for a new job midyear. She was replaced by a retired administrator who only worked part time.

*Stress Increased*

Anxieties rose, people felt overloaded, and weaknesses within the system became obvious. Like any remodel, human and materials costs were higher than anticipated, and implementation took longer than anyone thought possible.

*Relationships Were Challenged*

The leadership team was so busy planning within its grade-level teams that it found little time to meet and coordinate as a team. All faculty were so busy working with new team members that other long-standing relationships suffered. Students complained about missing friends who were in other teams. Students talked about "good" and "bad" teams. Some parents of "gifted" academic students objected to the reduction in tracking. Parents could no longer request a particular teacher; the request needed to be for a particular team. A few parents chose to send their students to other schools. In reality, many people who could see the need for change were so uncomfortable with the problems of the interim phase that they almost lost sight of the goal.

*Interim Changes and Doubts*

*"Are we sure it's going to be better?"* All teachers were working so hard that they felt dazed. Several teachers tried to renegotiate back to the old ways. Not all teachers chose to and/or were able to make the changes in teaching repertoire that would facilitate the mainstreaming of special needs students.

In reality, agreements and expectations were clear. Teams were given the authority to redesign curriculum, instruction, and assessment. There was not enough training in how to do so, however, particularly in how to do so in a collaborative process across disciplines.

*"I've been teaching this way for twenty years, and it works just fine."* This is the time when it is natural to question why you ever started. The vision has to be strong, as well as the commitment, to get through. At the beginning of the school year the number of D's and F's were at an all-time high. Many limited-English-speaking and special day class students were struggling so much that self-contained programs were allowed to reconstitute on a limited basis. With responsibilities of teams and administrators not clearly defined, student discipline became a major concern of staff. With the resignation of the assistant principal and the resulting extra burdens on the principal, staff questioned the leadership abilities of the principal. Teachers who had been most supportive of change became short-tempered and emotional at meetings as a result of the additional stress. Staff leaders were so busy in their own transition that they found little time to support each other or staff in need.

## Midway Through Year One: Living Through the Disruption

Old ways of doing things are no longer appropriate, and new ways are not yet in place.

In January 1993, the leadership team met after having read William Bridges's (1991) book. The team was particularly struck by Chapter 4 on the *neutral zone.* I attended this meeting and heard six people simultaneously shout, "This is where we are now!"

*Supporting the Vision and Each Other*

People continued to work longer and longer hours, attempting to make the restructuring efforts successful. When staff questioned the effectiveness of the student advisory program, the minority who wanted to disband it were outvoted. Instead, the staff brainstormed ways to make it work better. The district agreed to allow MHJHS to remain onsite for planning purposes on what were suppose to be districtwide inservice days. Teachers listened to and supported each other, verbally at meetings and emotionally one on one.

*Sorting and Reestablishing Priorities*

In early May, the leadership team started to meet again. This was the first time during the school year that so many staff members had reflected as a group on how the restructuring efforts were progressing. A list was made of all teachers who were clearly "on board." There was agreement that more than 50 percent were committed. The leadership team made lists of long- and short-term issues. Members consistently rechecked the principal's bottom line. The principal accepted responsibility for many of the unresolved issues related to managing the transition. The principal also stated that when the leadership team made decisions and he took them to the faculty, vocal support was important; the group agreed.

**Staff leaders to principal:** "You dropped the ball. We can't do this if you don't follow through with staff, district, and community!"

**Principal in response:** "You better be ready to back me up when I go to bat!"

*Recommitment to the Vision*

By the end of the year everyone was exhausted. We looked like "night of the living dead, survivors of the nuclear winter."

Ten teachers and the principal carefully planned the May 14 staff development day. During the day, the bilingual teacher, who had had a very difficult year, spontaneously stood up and started a "wave" that caught on with staff and eased tensions. The staff met in small groups and celebrated the positive accomplishments of the year and made public awards of recognition to individuals for their contributions to the year. It was at this time that the staff recommitted to the restructuring effort for 1993–1994, with the special note that this was only Year 1 of the five-year plan. It was clear that the remodel was too far along to consider turning back, and that almost everyone was pleased with some parts of the remodel. In the afternoon, a barbecue was held at the principal's house.

## Year Two—Best in the West

The leadership team recognized that a successful opening to the 1993–1994 school year was critical to maintain the teacher commitment to the restructuring efforts. At the same time, it recognized the need to begin to emerge from the neutral zone through a process that promised a higher quality of life for staff. The opening week of staff meetings prior to the return of students was planned carefully. A metaphor was needed to create a picture for the staff that would symbolize their work. It was agreed that this metaphor would be "best in the West." Agendas became trail guides; western music and decor set the scene; western gear was the dress code; and individual staff members shared the job of trail boss. These staff meetings were short, efficient, and productive. The result was a positive feeling among staff and a willingness to put extra effort into establishing a plan for positive student recognition and team recognition. For the opening district meeting, the entire staff dressed western, walked together from school to the meeting, and sat together. The statement to the rest of the school district was clear: Mission Hill stood together with pride; Mission Hill was the best in the West.

As the second year of implementation began, the leadership team agreed on two important priorities. First, the leadership team would meet regularly with the principal. Second, emphasis would be on fine-tuning, not adding new components. The components of the plan approved by the board more than a year earlier were coming into place; everyone had a stake in implementation. Consistency of staff/program support, morale, and team building were felt to be of utmost importance.

While the staff began the school year on an upbeat note, ongoing transition issues continued to affect morale throughout much of the school year. Resistance of a small minority of staff diminished the effectiveness of team efforts. Debates over tracking in math polarized some staff. Resistance became vocal, demanding a return to the old ways. However, more and more people across programs were feeling comfortable and talked about the positive difference in student attitudes. The majority demanded that new and different ways be found to solve remaining issues. New focus groups were formed, and a team-oriented school planning process was designed to build cohesiveness and a common vision for the future.

The issue of advisory became a focal point for complaints. Many staff saw this as one more responsibility, with little real payoff for students. At midyear, advisories were dropped as a result of a staff survey. This change improved staff morale by demonstrating to staff that frustrating components of the vision could be addressed and responded to positively. Additionally, it lightened the workload and simplified the weekly schedule.

## Preliminary Findings

There were indications that the changes were benefiting students. The campus was safer and cleaner. Discipline referrals were down 60 percent, and the suspension rate was down 70 percent. Graffiti on campus was sharply reduced, with only two serious cases during fall semester 1993. The academic success rate was also up, with the percentage of students passing all courses up from 75 percent to 85 percent.

## Year Three—The Sky's the Limit

During Year 3, several new components were added to the vision.

- Youth Serve, a service learning program for middle school students, was introduced at MHJHS, and approximately 200 students chose service learning as their seventh-period selective.
- A technology plan was developed. The computer lab was staffed. Community partnerships were fostered. Grant opportunities were pursued, several successfully.
- Schoolwide work began on student outcomes, rubrics, and evaluation processes that could be used in all classrooms.
- The principal gave his bottom line—integrated themes must be included in all core curriculum by each academic team. At least one research report was to be integrated across disciplines each year.

Problems continued, particularly around resistance from some members of the math department, frustrations with implementation of the seventh-period selectives program, and the desire for more funding.

## Year Four—Catch the Wave of Excellence

## Year Five—Set Sail with Mission Hill

At the end of Year 3, the principal accepted a position nearer his family in Texas. His growth as a school leader and his willingness to empower staff to be leaders were central to the success of the program during the previous three years. The new principal, although not new to the district, needed time to understand and become part of the MHJHS way. This is a common issue in school redesign. When a person central to the vision leaves, even when he is replaced by a person with excellent people and management skills, as was true in this case, the vision does not belong to this new person and the transition can be difficult for all parties.

Several setbacks took place. Public/parent perception of the selective program was not positive. Teachers who had repeatedly volunteered to teach selectives during seventh period were beginning to resent those teachers who did not volunteer. By the beginning of the fourth year, the coordinators of the selective program seriously questioned their capacity to find enough volunteers to provide classes for all students. At the semester, a compromise was found that reduced the selective program to only Tuesdays and Thursdays. Second, even though the math department agreed to utilize a new integrated math program, one math teacher continued to teach from the traditional book instead. Third, whereas many teachers were beginning to use the new school rubrics, many others were not, and there was no accountability.

At the same time, Years 4 and 5 saw important growth in availability and use of technology. The school was wired for technology during two net days, and considerable technology was added to the school. Considerable training was offered to teachers, and student use of technology in support of instruction occurred schoolwide.

## Year Six—Making Tracks

The original plan had been designed for five years. Year 6 was seen as a time to reassess. There was a general consensus that many things were going well. At the same time, it was clear to the leadership team that ownership of the school redesign was less tight than it had been in previous years. Several new staff members needed induction and support. Teachers were less consistent in enforcing schoolwide behavior expectations. A time-out room that teachers could use to deal with in-class behavior problems was eliminated for unrelated reasons, and student referrals to the assistant principal and the number of suspensions were going up.

Several important problems were identified. There was staff agreement that these problems could be addressed by giving people the opportunity to voice their concerns, that solutions could be reached by consensus, and that accountability for implementing these solutions was critical. One of these problems related to large class sizes. The superintendent agreed to give MHJHS two additional class sections for second semester in order to support the instructional priorities of the school and district.

A process was developed that would allow staff to discuss controversial issues and to reach consensus. The first topic selected was continuance of the seventh-period selective program. Many staff felt that students did not use this time constructively, that community volunteers were difficult to recruit and poor at classroom management, and that perhaps it was time to return this time to regular instructional minutes. Others disagreed, feeling that students did value this time, that the selectives were important, especially for English learning students and special education students who received tutorial support and for the many students who used the time for service learning or independent study, and that the problem was with implementation, not the concept. Students were surveyed. Results indicated strong student support.

I was asked to facilitate a staff meeting, utilizing the new consensus guidelines. Teachers in favor of the selective program did their homework. They presented the student survey results and had six students present the work they did during selective time. Prior to the meeting, they surveyed staff in order to understand and predict what the perceived concerns were and from whom. They came to the staff with proposals for dealing with each substantive concern. I helped the staff follow the agreed-upon process. At the end of two hours, all but two staff members voted to continue the selective program with agreed-upon modifications. Written evaluations of this meeting indicated that staff supported the process and that they wanted it used again for similar issues. I talked with several staff members six weeks later. They indicated that the

> MHJHS was more than half way through its sixth year of school redesign. Obviously, it has not been an easy process. Meaningful change never is. However, survey results of students, parents, and staff, as well as comments from most staff, indicate a deep commitment to what is happening for students. Only a handful of staff would argue for a return to the old. The vast majority just wish that transition wasn't such hard work.

modifications had been implemented, and that staff were pleased with the how the selective program was progressing.

In March, the staff was presented with the results of the yearly parent survey (see "Student Outcomes") and with results of a related staff survey. The school vision statement, the six school-wide student outcomes, and the 1997–1998 goals were revisited in light of the data found in these two surveys. Consensus was reached on goals for 1998–1999, and each staff member publicly committed to being on at least one of the task forces formed around each goal. I was present during this three-hour meeting. The process was skillfully facilitated by the leadership team. Staff felt good about progress being made this year, were open to areas identified for improvement, and reached consensus easily about goals for the next year. I was particularly impressed by the quality and honesty of the brainstorming in evaluating the vision, student outcomes, and current year goals and by the number of staff who were involved in planning and facilitating this process.

## Background

MHJHS is one of two seventh- and eighth-grade schools within the Santa Cruz City School District. The enrollment is 545, 24 percent Hispanic, 66 percent white, not Hispanic, 4 percent African-American, 4 percent Asian, 2 percent other. Ten and one-half percent are English language learners, speaking eleven languages other than English. Seven percent receive free or reduced price meals.

I served as a high school principal in this district for fourteen years. There has been a long-standing commitment to shared decision making and to support for school change. When I was hired in 1977, there were parents, students, teachers, classified staff, and administrators on the interview panel. This practice of broad input into all hiring decisions was and still is an expectation. Each school has a budget committee consisting of teachers, classified staff, parents and, on the secondary level, students to advise the principal. Since 1978 each school has had a school site council consisting of teachers, classified staff, parents, the principal, and, on the secondary level, students to develop and monitor a school plan for program improvement. In 1988 Santa Cruz was the first school district in the country, I think, to offer tenured teachers the option of developing their own professional development plan collaboratively with peers in lieu of formal evaluation (Krovetz & Cohick, 1993). This practice has become an increasingly popular option within numerous school districts in this region.

## Student Outcomes

*Parent Survey*

The results of the 1998 parent survey were published comparing survey results for 1996, 1997, and 1998. Two areas of focus for the 1997–1998 school year had been technology and school safety. Regarding technology, parents rated the three questions regarding technology increasingly more favorably over the three years—student computer proficiency, computer access, and amount of useful equipment. Regarding school safety, parents rated three questions more favorably for 1998 than for the previous two years—safety in school (81 percent satisfied), safety in classes (90 percent satisfied) and safety on yard (81 percent satisfied). Regarding the instructional program, parents were very satisfied with the science program (83 percent satisfied), math program (83 percent satisfied), physical education program (90 percent satisfied), and increasingly satisfied with the humanities program (72 percent satisifed, up from 63 percent in 1996). Eighty percent of parents were satisfied with how parents were included in the school, 77 percent were satisfied with school spirit, and 70 percent with extracurricular activities. Parents were also increasingly satisfied with school responsiveness to individual and cultural differences (73 percent satisfied, up from 43 percent satisfied in 1996). Many schools would be excited with these results and not reflect more deeply. At MHJHS however, the voices of parents, students, and staff are relied on to guide practice.

There were several areas for concern. Parents were concerned about level of challenge (60 percent satisfied, down from 72 percent in 1996) and homework (62.5 percent satisfied, down from 68 percent in 1996). Also, parents seemed to have less understanding of the family team organizational pattern for the school (73 percent satisfied in 1998, down from 79 percent in 1996). Parents were concerned about the selective program (57 percent satisfied satisfied, down form 62 percent in 1996) and with the availability of extra help for students (57 percent satisfied, down from 64 percent in 1996). The survey was administered prior to the adjustments in the selective program. The others areas of concern were addressed by staff in setting goals for the next year.

Results were based on responses from 173 families.

*Staff Survey*

All teachers were surveyed based on goals within the school plan. Results were reported for seventh-grade core teachers, eighth-grade core teachers and schoolwide elective teachers. These results were also looked at in detail in evaluating current practice and in setting priorities for the next year.

*California Achievement Test (CAT) 5 (Norm-Referenced Test)*

Using the results from 1996 and 1997, staff agreed that language mechanics and expression would be focus areas for the 1997–1998 school year. Core teachers have increased attention to these areas. California has mandated a different test for 1998, but there is a commitment to use the results from this new test to check on progress in the designated areas and to inform practice for the following year.

## Final Thought

One area that the school needs to improve on is using actual student work to guide decision making. The school rubrics are available to serve as a guide. At one time, there was staff agreement that these rubrics would be used schoolwide. The rubrics need to be revisited by staff, agreements need to be recommitted to, and accountability procedures need to be put into place.

## Update Written Winter 2006–2007

In 1998 the principal left Mission Hill to return to Texas. Since that time, there have been four principals and eight assistant principals. Many teachers, including several key teacher leaders, retired. The district is experiencing declining enrollment and in 2003 closed two elementary schools and added sixth grade to

Mission Hill. The small learning community structure at seventh and eighth grade no longer exists. This was caused by declining enrollment, the related decline in staffing, and therefore the inability to staff two full small learning committees cleanly at each grade level. Mission Hill has been labeled a Performance Improvement School.

On the teacher workday opening the 2006-2007 school year, an experienced teacher and the current principal led an all-faculty history wall activity. All teachers had Post-its. They wrote down significant, positive things that had happened since they arrived at Mission Hill and placed the Post-its on chart paper that had been taped up along a twenty-foot wall. The chart paper was labeled chronologically from the year that the most senior teacher started at Mission Hill (1970) to 2006. Following a gallery walk, they lined up in front of the chart paper at the year when they first came to Mission Hill. Of thirty-four faculty members, six lined up in the period 2000 and before, a large group lined up in front of 2003 as they came when the sixth grade was added, and a large group lined up in front of 2005 or 2006. I was in attendance.

I scheduled an initial meeting with the group of six who had been at the school the longest. We met about six weeks after the school year began. Also in attendance was a classified employee who is the site program coordinator for categorical programs, runs the school computer lab, is a very strong leader in the school community, and started at the school in 1978. In preparation, I asked them to reread the original case study, and I reminded them that the focus had been on the change process at Mission Hill. I have visited the school numerous times in recent years; the teacher who led the history wall activity was recently a student in the San Jose State University master's program in collaborative leadership, and I had supervised her fieldwork.

When I entered the school for the interviews, the first thing that I saw was the large amount of student work, primarily science reports, that filled the first-floor hallways. The large bulletin boards were about student activities and student learning, with a clear focus on issues of equity and diversity. Antibullying, advantages of being bilingual, and teaching tolerance posters were up in several places. Student writing about tolerance took up much of the hallway on the second floor. I did not see any focus on negative student behavior. I did not see any posting about what students should NOT be doing. I was struck by the very positive message that was being given to students about student work, student learning, and student relationships.

I asked the seven staff members to talk with me about what was left from the change efforts of the 1990s. The immediate response from all seven was that despite the changes in administration and staff, the focus continues to be on what is best for students. They talked sadly about the loss of the small learning communities and the reasons for this—declining enrollment and therefore reduced number of teaching positions, the need for most teachers to teach at more than one grade level, and also how the credentialing laws made it harder for a teacher to teach in more than one discipline. They talked about the continuing collaboration among a group of strong teacher-leaders who supported administration and encouraged communication among all staff members. They also talked about the impact of having so many new teachers, and how most of them never experienced and therefore could not appreciate the quality of collaboration that occurred in the past. During the 2003–2004 school year teachers worked to contract almost all year due to union-district inability to reach a contract agreement. Therefore, much of the common collaboration time and preparation time for collaboration was not used at a time that coincided with many new teachers joining the faculty as sixth-grade teachers. At one staff meeting that year, there was conversation about what *work to contract* meant. Newer teachers voiced that weekly common planning time was for individual teacher preparation. More experienced teachers explained that the time was set aside by teacher initiative in order for teachers to have time to collaborate. In 2006–2007, grade-level team meetings are honing in constructive conversations about specific students and meeting their learning needs. There is an agreement that teams of teachers will meet with a parent when the meeting is to talk about meeting the student's learning needs.

They talked about how several of the previous principals did not appreciate the importance of collaboration and how teacher-leaders had to fight for department time and cross department time for collaboration. They agreed that the current principal is supportive of time for collaboration. They talked about the increased districtwide focus on professional development, especially on meeting the needs of English language learners, and the fine balance that occurs, with limited time available, between meetings that are all-district and the need for site-level collaboration time to meet the needs of the specific students at Mission Hill. They talked about how the math department was tracking students more in response to wanting to raise achievement and how tracking in math impacts students' schedules throughout their day. One of the teachers said, "The hardest thing is the big turnover of staff and how to hold on to the vision of why we are here and why we do what we do." In response, the teacher who has been at the school the longest said, "The foundation of the change effort has not altered. We are here for kids. Education of kids comes first, and collaboration is about supporting our students."

Under the new principal, hired in January 2006, a functioning leadership team (LT) has been reinstituted. The principal, assistant principal, and interested teachers are invited to attend. Norms and a clear decision-making process have been instituted. The LT meets once a month before the monthly staff meeting. Since staff knows that the LT makes decisions, many teachers attend each meeting. This has helped empower new teachers, as their voices are valued in this process.

I have known the principal for many years. She was the assistant principal at Mission Hill when the change process began. She left for a number of years and has returned as principal. One day when I came to talk with her, two ninth-grade Latino students were in her office saying hello. They are now high school students, and they come to say hello and check in with her on a regular basis. The conversation was about the high expectations that she has for both students.

She talked with me about how in many ways 2006–2007 is like the late 1980s at Mission Hill. There are many new teachers. There is a new principal. Shared decision making and teacher leadership is again becoming a valued part of the school. And, the school has recognized the need to focus on the unique learning needs of the English language learning students. She recognizes that the achievement gap is large and is working to address it. She mentioned three initiatives. First, the district is focused on building the capacity of teachers to be more successful with English language learners and is allocating time and money to support this initiative. On a monthly basis, teachers are taught specific strategies proven to work with English language learning students and are expected to practice them. Initially, this professional development was led by district and site administrators. The leadership has passed to teacher-leaders who develop subject-specific professional development based on teacher needs. Second, a Latino parent has become very active in the school, working closely with the principal and the English language development staff to engage other Latino parents. Latino parents are attending school meetings; messages home, including the all-call phone-message system, are in English and Spanish; Latino parents are saying they feel a part of the school. Third, programs are being put in place to support these students, and the effectiveness of these programs is being evaluated. The school now has an AVID program and support classes in Power Math (critical thinking), reading, and writing to support students in their mainstream classes. The principal talked with me about ways in which these programs were effective and areas of concern that demonstrated her first hand knowledge of how the programs are being implemented. As it needs to be, her ultimate goal is to improve learning for all students, and she recognizes that one key component of measuring that is raising the test scores, especially for the English language learning students.

## Final Thought

In the NCLB world, Mission Hill, like so many other schools, has its work cut out for it. The bar will be raised in 2007–2008, with substantially higher student achievement being required to avoid being labeled Program Improvement or to get off that list, as is the case for Mission Hill. If administrators and staff stay at Mission Hill and remain focused as a community on closing the achievement gap, they will be successful.

### Mission Hill Middle School
425 King ST
Santa Cruz, CA 95060
831-429-3860
Web site: www.missionhill.santacruz.k12.ca.us

**Enrollment:**            **578**
Hispanic                   25.4%
White (not Hispanic)       59.5%
African American           3.1%
Asian                      4.7%

| API | 1999 | 2005 | 2006 | Change |
|---|---|---|---|---|
| Total | 735 | 769 | 786 | + 51 |
| Hispanic | 530 | 644 | 634 | +104 |
| White (not Hispanic) | 806 | 829 | 859 | + 53 |

# CHAPTER EIGHT

# Marty Krovetz's Top-Ten List of Commonly Asked Questions About Resilience

## QUESTION 10: OUR STAFF IS VERY CONGENIAL, AND WE ARE KNOWN FOR HOW CARING WE ARE WITH STUDENTS. AREN'T WE DOING RESILIENCE ALREADY?

Resilience is not something you "do," it is something you "are." Look back at Chapter 2, particularly Figure 2.1. Your staff may care deeply, but does your staff truly believe in the ability of all students to develop the habits of mind to learn to use their hearts and minds well? Are there high expectations and purposeful support, or does caring mean that you expect less because "students are so needy?" How are student, staff, and community voices valued in the school? What specific evidence can you provide in answering these questions? A careful assessment of your school's practices would be informative.

Second, *congenial* means getting along well. *Collegial* is very different. Collegial refers to the ways people support each other to be more effective professionals.

## QUESTION 9: HOW CAN WHAT HAPPENS IN MY CLASSROOM OR IN MY SCHOOL OVERCOME THE PROBLEMS MY STUDENTS ENCOUNTER OUTSIDE OF SCHOOL?

Bonnie Benard (2003) writes, "Resilience studies provide critical information to closing the achievement gap, because they give educators clear evidence that all children and youth have the capacity to be educated, and that teachers and schools do have the power to educate them successfully."

You know from your own daily experiences that some of your students who come from high-risk backgrounds are successful in school. Many others find success later in their lives. We know from Emmy Werner and Ruth Smith's research, and again from our own experiences, that students who are successful usually have known an adult who really cared about them, have had people hold high expectations for them and support them to meet these expectations, and have had people value their participation; they have had reason to be hopeful about their future. I do not mean to diminish the importance of family and community, but the basis for resilience is that what you do or do not do influences the lives of your students. We all have had people enter our lives briefly who have had an influence on how we view our future. You may want to reread the inspirational words of Mervlyn Kitashima in Chapter 4.

## QUESTION 8: WHAT IS THE ROLE OF THE DISTRICT OFFICE IN FOSTERING RESILIENCE?

Resilience is fostered throughout school districts when central office personnel see their primary function as supporting school efforts, as opposed to seeing school efforts supporting district initiatives.

Primarily, the superintendent and other district office personnel can model behaviors that foster resilience for the adults in the schools. This includes helping the school focus on a very limited number of important priorities, including resilience; helping to provide resources to accomplish these priorities; recognizing and rewarding collaborative efforts to accomplish these priorities; valuing student outcomes that are related to students using their minds and hearts well; holding school personnel accountable for helping all students achieve a limited number of important student outcomes; expecting each school community to make decisions about curriculum, budget, hiring, and professional development that affect the daily workings of that school; including the participation of school people in important district decisions; making sure that all district departments/personnel respond quickly and efficiently to school requests; and maintaining good relations with the teacher and classified unions. The manner in which district office personnel interact with and respond to school personnel has a major impact on the climate of individual schools.

## QUESTION 7: HOW DO WE COACH OUR PRINCIPAL SO THAT SHE SEES THE BUILDING OF A RESILIENT LEARNING COMMUNITY AS A PRIORITY?

First, you need to share the ideas of resilience with your principal. She should read Bonnie Benard's 1991 article and this book at a minimum. Second, you need to help the principal see that building a resilient learning community will further the vision and goals she has for the school. It is imperative that the principal view fostering resilience as a critical support for her priorities. Third, you need to convince your principal that building a resilient learning community is doable for your school with existing resources and with existing staff. Fourth, you need to have the courage to help lead the effort.

## QUESTION 6: HOW CAN WE CREATE CHANGE IN INDIVIDUAL TEACHERS ABOUT ATTITUDES AND EXPECTATIONS TOWARD CERTAIN GROUPS OF STUDENTS, SUCH AS TITLE 1, ENGLISH LANGUAGE LEARNING, MIGRANT, AND SPECIAL EDUCATION?

In many schools, this can be difficult. Teachers are often used to these students being served in pull-out programs by specialists. They do not feel prepared to teach these students and do not see it as their responsibility. Most research supports inclusion. Quality professional development and resource allocation support is needed to bolster this effort.

In my opinion, there are two ways to proceed. For the first option, the district, principal, and/or staff decides that inclusion will occur for these students, and that adequate resources, especially time, and professional development are allocated to support teacher development in order to help assure the success of these students and these teachers. Remember that teachers need to feel successful or they will lower their expectations for students and for themselves. Therefore, high expectations and purposeful support should be high priorities for both teachers and students.

For the second option, win teachers over one at a time. You and other leaders need to share the research with individual teachers, knowing that by itself research will not convince others. You also need to demonstrate to the teacher, that with your support, a limited number of students can be included in that teacher's classroom and that these students can be successful. You will probably need to twist arms, put your relationship on the line, and take this teacher to classrooms in which these students are being successful. You will need to share successes and strategies that have proven effective for you. You will need to take risks and be persistent.

## QUESTION 5: HOW DO YOU GET A MATURE STAFF THAT HAS A HISTORY OF MISTRUST AND PRIVATE PRACTICE TO TALK WITH EACH OTHER ABOUT FOSTERING RESILIENCE?

Head on! Most certificated and classified staff members want to work in a school that fosters resilience for students and particularly for themselves. The many compromises made over the years wear school people out. This is understandable, and not their fault! Maintain a clear focus on what is in it for staff as well as for students. In my experience, most staffs respond very positively to talk about resilience because fostering resilience is at the heart of what most adults want in their own lives and relates so directly to why they entered teaching as a career.

Reread and follow the suggestions in Chapter 7. Mission Hill Middle High School had been a mature staff with a history of mistrust and private practice. It changed because of excellent teacher, staff, and administrative leadership, careful planning, time, and patience.

## QUESTION 4: HOW WILL WE KNOW WE ARE SUCCEEDING IN FOSTERING RESILIENCE? WHAT MEASURES WOULD WE USE? WHO WOULD WE USE THEM WITH? WHEN WOULD WE USE THEM?

These are important questions often asked by Emmy Werner. We would expect that, if a school is increasingly fostering resilience, students should be able to demonstrate increased social competence, problem-solving skills, autonomy, and sense of purpose and future. One key question then is can students graduating from your school demonstrate increasing competence in each of these four areas? To determine this, tasks should be designed, with teacher, student, and community input, that students would complete in order to demonstrate their competence. Students should also be held accountable to high standards of literacy and habits of mind, both of which are required in order to demonstrate competence in the four areas. Of course, purposeful support should be provided as needed. Reread "Graduation by Exhibition" at Anzar High School in Chapter 1.

In addition, at a minimum, schools should collect the following data:

- Standardized test score data—Whether we like these tests or not, we should expect students to demonstrate increased competence in reading, writing, and mathematics. Our public expects achievement in these areas.
- Longitudinal data—We should exam student work, attitudes and behaviors over the time the student is in our school in order to guide decisions about individual student's learning needs, as well as to determine program effectiveness. We should also conduct meaningful follow up after the student leaves, so that long-term effects can be documented and learned from.
- Survey data—Tools used initially to assess the resilience of your school should be administered to staff, parents, and students over time in order to learn about perceived changes in your school's culture.

As I state in Chapter 7, school redesign efforts will not be sustained over time if we do not make good decisions based on sound data.

## QUESTION 3: SHOULD WE TEACH STUDENTS ABOUT RESILIENCE AND HELP THEM UNDERSTAND HOW TO FOSTER RESILIENCE IN THEMSELVES?

The answer is yes, but recognize that this is not sufficient. It would be useful for students to understand resilience and to learn ways to seek situations that foster their own resilience. However, one should be building a school culture based on fostering resilience and consider teaching students about resilience as only one of several initiatives.

## QUESTION 2: GIVEN THE PRESSURE OF NCLB, HOW DO WE FIND TIME AND RESOURCES TO FOSTER RESILIENCE?

This commonly asked question was answered in Chapter 3:

1. Being caring and respectful means guaranteeing as much as we can that every child can read, write, and compute;

2. Being caring and respectful means holding high expectations for every child regardless of race, ethnicity, gender, economic status, sexual preference, or learning handicap;

3. If we want children to be caring and compassionate, then we must provide schools that model caring and compassion.

I like what Herb Waxman, Jon Gray, and Yolanda Padron (2004) write about NCLB.

Resiliency education is not only aligned with the objectives of the No Child Left Behind Act (NCLB), it provides the means for the essential achievement of that legislation—effectively addressing the specific problems and local conditions of the culturally and linguistically diverse minority students that are in danger of being left behind. This legislation has enabled educators to focus on what can be done to reduce the achievement gap between white and minority students and high- and low-income students. By focusing on students' strengths, educational resilience provides an important foundation for promoting excellence for *all* students. (p. 4)

## QUESTION 1: I AM EXHAUSTED. HOW DO I FOSTER RESILIENCE FOR MYSELF?

This is the most common issue raised by beginning administrators in my classes. I am certainly not the best role model for this. As a former high school principal and now as a university professor I work sixty-plus hour weeks, eat on the run, and could do a much better job of caring for myself. I do have some "do as I say, not as I do" suggestions, however. They are listed in no particular order.

- Control your own calendar, and write in time for exercise and family on a weekly and daily basis.
- Control your calendar, and write in time to do the work related things that bring you joy.
- Develop a professional support group that you meet with at least every other week; breakfast meetings are easier to keep to a manageable length than end-of-day meetings.
- Recruit a mentor who you respect to coach you through stressful times and to serve as a sounding board in order to have fewer stressful times.
- Attend professional counseling on a regular basis.
- Keep paper by your bed to write notes on when thoughts about school business wake you up.
- Learn to delegate properly and to trust in others to do the best they know how.
- Learn to discern what's important from what's not important. Only do things well that need to be done well. Many of the tasks given to us just need to be done or can be filed until someone reminds us to do them.
- Don't let personnel issues fester. Deal with them skillfully, now.
- Don't take attacks on your ideas personally. Relish the intellectual discourse you create, and tell people if they respond to you personally rather than to your ideas.
- Whenever you have a long weekend or vacation, leave town.
- Live near your work; do not miss dinners and events that focus on your family.
- As often as possible, say that you have a commitment that you cannot change when someone, particularly your supervisor, wants to meet with you on very short notice.
- Hold most school conversations standing.
- Be honest; it is too stressful to be someone other than yourself.

CHAPTER NINE

# A Final Word
# or Two

Ending as we began:

> "How do you like my school?" asked María.
> "I'm very impressed by how friendly everyone is," said I.
> ***"More important, they really trust me here," said María.***

Schools that really trust their students—schools that value, respect, and know their students—are schools that foster resilience for their students. Such schools are full of adults who believe that all students are capable of learning the habits of mind to use their minds and hearts well. These adults understand how important it is for student learning and for student hopefulness that all students know that they are cared about, that expectations are high, that purposeful support is in place, and that their participation is valued.

To be so for students, schools must also be full of adults who value, respect and know each other well. Adults must believe that they and their colleagues are capable of learning the habits of mind to use their minds and hearts well. Resilience factors need to be in place for the adults as well as for the students.

Few schools are full of adults who share these beliefs. However, within your community and mine there are schools that are striving to be resilient learning communities. I hope that this book will encourage you to be a part of the very important work these schools are so courageously doing and to help other schools undertake their journeys.

# Resources

## RESOURCE A

**For each bullet, rate that item on a 1 to 4 scale:**
**1 = Not present in classrooms or on campus**
**2 = Seen in classrooms or on campus but does not stand out**
**3 = Evident in classrooms and/or on campus**
**4 = Clearly a part of the classroom and school culture**

### Caring

What would a school look like whose culture is centered on caring?

1.  Sense of belonging
    - Students talk freely about feeling respected, supported, and known by teachers, administrators, and peers.
    - Teachers and classified staff talk easily about feeling respected, valued, supported, and known by administrators, peers, students, and parents. (Ask the custodian.)
    - Teachers and classified staff feel included in discussions and decision making.
    - Office staff is friendly and courteous to students, staff, parents, community, and visitors.
    - Body language in the halls and in classrooms is unanxious—students are not afraid of other students; student body language does not change when adults approach.

2.  Cooperation is promoted
    - Cross-age tutoring programs are in place to support student learning.

- Cooperative learning is taught and practiced in classes.
- Conflict resolution skills are taught and practiced throughout the school.
- Students are seen mixing easily across race, ethnicity, and gender.

3. Celebration of successes is practiced
   - Lots of students, teachers, staff, parents, and community members are recognized for their contributions in a wide variety of ways.
   - People use the word "we" when talking about the school.
   - Positive communications go home from teachers and administrators regularly.
   - People talk openly about what didn't work and what was learned.

4. Leaders spend lots of positive time with members
   - Administrators are seen interacting with students in positive ways.
   - Administrators know and use the names of all or most students.
   - Teachers, students, parents, and staff talk about the principal seeming to be everywhere.
   - Class continues when administrators walk in.

5. Resources are obtained with a minimum of effort
   - The campus is clean and orderly.
   - There are lots of books in classrooms.
   - Teachers report that the office staff is supportive of their teaching.
   - The supply closet is open and copy machines are readily available.
   - The library and computers are accessible to students, teachers, staff, parents before and after school and during recess.

What would curriculum, instruction, and assessment be like in a school that is centered on caring?

*Curriculum*

- The work is meaningful to the students; students can tell you what they are doing and why; when asked, students will say that what they are learning is meaningful and meets their current and future life needs.
- Curriculum is integrated and thematic and focuses on a limited number of important content standards.
- Curriculum respects and acknowledges the ethnography and community of the students, using this as a departure point for curriculum that explores diversity of culture and opinion within and without the community.
- Students have choices in what they learn (curriculum), how they learn (instruction), and how they present what they have learned (assessment).

*Instruction*

- Students are working and teachers are coaching; that is students are actively engaged in work. I like the thought that students should work at least as hard as their teachers.
- Teachers move around the room and talk with individual students or with small groups of students.
- Students spend extended periods with the same teacher and with the same students.
- Time is provided for teachers to work together on developing instructional strategies, including peer coaching.

*Assessment*

- Student work is displayed throughout the school.
- Students know and can articulate expectations teachers have for student learning. Most often rubrics are assessable and have been developed with student input.
- Students can be seen presenting what they have learned to others.
- Students have opportunities to demonstrate what they learn in meaningful ways, including self-reflection and participation in their own performance review.

What do teacher and administrator roles look like in a school focused on caring?

1. Decision making
   - Important decisions are made in a collaborative manner, involving all stakeholders in the decisions; one seldom hears, "We can't," "We aren't allowed," "I wasn't told." "I was told I have to ..." "It's his or her fault."
   - Meetings designed to make decisions set aside adequate time for reflection, discussion, consensus building, and planning for action.
   - Ground rules for decision making are agreed upon, known, followed, and regularly reassessed.
   - Conflict resolution strategies have been agreed upon, are taught, and are practiced.

2. Student discipline
   - Expectations for student behavior are reasonable, positive, public, known and enforced with consistency.
   - Classroom discipline is dealt with primarily by the classroom teacher; there are very few referrals to the office for disrespect.
   - The school disciplinarian does not spend the majority of his or her time disciplining students; rather he or she spends considerable time working positively with teachers, students, parents, and community.
   - Student discipline is done privately, in a problem-solving mode.

3. Teacher as advisor
   - A strong student advisory system is in place. Advisories will not work in schools where teachers are responsible for large numbers of students.
   - Teachers maintain regular contact with parents regarding student progress, including positive feedback.
   - Teachers maintain regular contact with their students other teachers. The school is organized in ways to support this communication.
   - Teachers, parents, and students collaborate to develop an individual learning plan for each student.

4. Teacher as collaborator
- Teachers can be seen working in a collegial school culture—adults talk with one another, observe one another, help one another, laugh together, and celebrate together.
- Conversations in the faculty room are lively, with teachers talking positively about students, student work, their own work, and the work of colleagues.
- Faculty and staff are not seen brooding in the faculty room or in the parking lot or segregated by sex, race, department, or age.
- Time and resources are provided for teachers to collaborate.
- People talk openly about what didn't work and what was learned.

## High Expectations and Purposeful Support

- Reasonable, positive, public, consistently enforced policies and procedures are in place. Optimally, students are involved in drafting, evaluating, and revising these policies.
- The campus is well maintained with little litter and graffiti.
- A broad range of student work is on display throughout the school.
- Teachers are heard talking about individual students and their work and ways to proactively support that student's learning.
- Every student can name at least two adults who know him or her well and his or her work well.
- Students are seen working together on school projects.
- Students are seen tutoring other students inside and outside the classroom.
- The parents' and extended family's roles in supporting student learning are valued and supported through parent and grandparent workshops, a parent library, and availability of social services support. Such roles are also supported by proactively seeking and utilizing the knowledge and skills of the family as a resource in the school, classroom, and curriculum.

- Members of the community are seen mentoring students. Research by the Public/Private Ventures in Philadelphia found that kids enrolled in Big Brothers and Big Sisters were 52 percent less likely to skip school than a matched control group, 33 percent less likely to exhibit violent behavior, and 46 percent less likely to try drugs for the first time. Enrolled African American youth were 70 percent less likely to try drugs (Butler, 1997).
- Programs proven to support student achievement and sense of belonging are highly visible on campus such as Advancement Via Individual Determination (AVID; www.avi donline.org), Link Crew (www.linkcrew.com), Reading Recovery (www.readingrecovery.org), Asset Development (www.search-institute.org), and Tribes (www.tribes.com).
- Teachers, parents, and students talk openly about the commitment of the principal and district to all students learning to use their minds and hearts well.
- Staff articulate a common mission that all agree transcends personal differences.

What would curriculum, instruction, and assessment be like in a school that is designed to foster high expectations and purposeful support for all students?

*Curriculum*

- Students are actively engaged in interdisciplinary, thematic, project-based work that is based on a limited number of important content standards.
- Projects have significance to students and are based on important questions raised by students, teachers, and community members.
- Curriculum respects and acknowledges the ethnography and community of the students, using this as a departure point for curriculum that explores diversity of culture and opinion within and without the community.
- Teachers differentiate curriculum that addresses learning styles and special needs of students.
- Students comment (or proudly complain) that the work is challenging and takes time.

*Instruction*

- Classes are heterogeneously grouped for most of the day, with regrouping as appropriate.
- Students usually are working in small groups or independently.
- Well-defined safety nets are in place to accelerate students who are falling behind in their academic progress. Students are required to participate in these safety nets in order to accelerate their learning. Safety nets are regularly evaluated for their effectiveness.
- When teachers ask questions, students are required to use higher-order thinking skills to answer and all students have equal access to respond; when students ask questions, teachers usually reply with a question that requires thought by the student, rather than with the answer.
- Teachers differentiate instruction to addresses the need of all students.

*Assessment*

- Student learning is assessed in a variety of ways, including the use of well-publicized rubrics, public exhibitions, and self-reflection by students.
- Individual teachers use assessment strategies on a daily basis to diagnose the learning of individual students and to adjust and differentiate instruction based on this assessment.
- Teachers review student work and other assessment data together to guide school and classroom practice.
- When asked, students talk articulately about their best work.

What do teacher and administrator roles look like in such a school?

- The principal knows students and student work well and is often seen engaged in conversations with teachers about individual students and their learning.
- Teachers and school and district administrators have agreed on best practices in a limited number of areas of focus (literacy, habits of mind), and time, resources, and professional development are supporting implementation—including expert and peer coaching and collaborative action research.

- Time is provided for teachers to discuss the needs and successes of individual students.
- Time is provided for teachers to review student work and other school data together and discuss implications of this data for improving classroom practice.
- Teachers talk openly about how supportive the principal and district are regarding supporting ideas and helping to provide resources.
- Teachers seek out parents as partners in supporting the learning of students and, in particular, contact parents regularly when students are doing well.

## Meaningful Participation

What would a school look like whose culture is centered on meaningful participation by all students?

- Students are working in the library, computer lab, laboratories, and hallways, individually and collaboratively with peers.
- Students are engaged in required helpfulness.
- Older students are seen working with younger students.
- Students are engaged with peers as peer helpers, conflict resolvers, and tutors;
- Students spend time each week in service learning projects on and off campus.
- Class meetings and schoolwide forums are held regularly to gather student input regarding meaningful school issues. These meetings are often facilitated by students.
- An effort is being made to include all student groups in the daily life of the school; students are not seen on the fringes of the school campus, alienated and voicing displeasure with the school, staff, and peers.
- A large percentage of the students participate in and lead a wide range of school activities.
- Signs on campus encourage students to join activities and do not indicate hurdles to complete; the words "students must" do not appear on school postings.
- Time is provided at least weekly for teachers to work together on curriculum, instruction, and assessment.

- Most students, faculty, and staff are known and welcomed by name, and many parents and community members are known and welcomed by name.
- Drug, alcohol, smoking, and fighting infractions are statistically small and show an annual decrease.

What would curriculum, instruction and assessment be like in a school designed to foster meaningful participation by all students?

*Curriculum*

- Curriculum is project based, set around complex issues, some of which relate to school and community issues.
- Student work is posted throughout the school.
- Students have choices in the specifics of what they investigate, how they do the investigation, and how they demonstrate what they have learned.
- Service learning is a part of every student's academic program.

*Instruction*

- Teachers ask students questions that require students to do critical, reflective thinking such as the questions associated with Anzar and CPESS's Habits of Mind.
- Teachers spend much of their time coaching students, and students spend much of their time working individually and in small groups.
- Students are actively engaged in lessons; they are not seen sitting unengaged in the back of classrooms.
- School resources are readily available; computers and resource materials are easy for students to access.

*Assessment*

- Students exhibit and reflect on what they have learned.
- Standards for quality work are well known and often designed with student input. Rubrics are created jointly by teachers and students.
- Teachers use student work to guide classroom and school practices.
- Student exhibitions are regularly shared schoolwide and with the community.

What do teacher and administrator roles look like in such a school?

- Principals, teachers, students, parents, community members, and classified staff are engaged in schoolwide decision making around issues of substance, including establishing school priorities, budgeting to support those priorities, and hiring of personnel.
- Norms for decision making, consensus building, and conflict resolution are mutually agreed upon, followed, and regularly reassessed.
- Meetings focus on meaningful input and decision making rather than information giving; agendas are posted with opportunities for agenda input; relevant information is provided ahead of meetings; participants are at meetings on time; meetings start on time and end on time.
- Divergent thinking is encouraged and heard in formal meetings and informal conversations.
- Conversations and comments reflect respect for others, in and out of meetings. Put downs, side conversations, and comments that indicate exclusion are not heard in or out of meetings.
- Mistakes are celebrated as learning experiences, and responsibility for mistakes are shared without blame.
- Teachers work collegially, sharing curriculum and instructional strategies, talking about students and student work, and coaching each other to be more effective. Time and resources are provided to support this.
- Teachers talk freely about feeling valued by administrators, staff, parents, and students as participants in the whole school community.
- Administrators, faculty, classified staff, students, and parents seem to enjoy being together; across roles, people seek each other out, talk together, laugh together.
- Faculty and staff are not seen complaining, blaming, or brooding in the faculty room or in the parking lot.
- Students are given classroom and schoolwide responsibilities of increasing importance with age.

# RESOURCE B

## Assessing School Resiliency Building
(from Henderson & Milstein, 1996)

Evaluate the following elements of school resiliency building using a scale of 1 to 4, with 1 indicating "we have this together," 2 indicating "we've done a lot in this area, but could do more," 3 indicating "we are getting started," and 4 indicating "nothing has been done."

*Prosocial Bonding*

\_\_\_ *Students* have a positive bond with at least one caring adult in the school.
\_\_\_ *Students* are engaged in lots of interest-based before-, after-, and during-school activities
\_\_\_ *Staff* engages in meaningful interactions with one another.
\_\_\_ *Staff* has been involved in creating meaningful vision and mission statements.
\_\_\_ Families are positively bonded to the *school*.
\_\_\_ The physical environment of the *school* is warm, positive, and inviting.
\_\_\_ TOTAL SCORE

*Clear, Consistent Boundaries*

\_\_\_ *Students* are clear about the behaviors expected of them and experience consistency in boundary enforcement.
\_\_\_ *Students* use an intervention process ("core" or "care" team) that helps them when they are having problems.
\_\_\_ *Staff* is clear about what is expected of them and experience consistency of expectations.
\_\_\_ *Staff* models the behavioral expectations developed for students and for adults.
\_\_\_ The *school* fosters an ongoing discussion of norms, rules, goals, and expectations for staff and students.
\_\_\_ The *school* provides training necessary for members of the school community to effectively set and live by behavioral expectations.
\_\_\_ TOTAL SCORE

*Teaching Life Skills*

\_\_\_\_    *Students* use refusal skills, assertiveness, healthy conflict resolution, good decision making and problem solving, and healthy stress-management skills most of the time.

\_\_\_\_    *Students* are engaged in cooperative learning that focuses on both social skills and academic outcomes.

\_\_\_\_    *Staff* works cooperatively together and emphasizes the importance of cooperation.

\_\_\_\_    *Staff* has the interpersonal skills necessary to engage in effective organizational functioning and the professional skills necessary for effective teaching.

\_\_\_\_    The *school* provides the skill development needed by all members of the school community.

\_\_\_\_    The *school* promotes a philosophy of lifelong learning.

\_\_\_\_    TOTAL SCORE

*Caring and Support*

\_\_\_\_    *Students* feel cared for and supported in the school.

\_\_\_\_    *Students* experience many types of incentives, recognitions, and rewards.

\_\_\_\_    *Staff* feels cared for and appreciated in the school.

\_\_\_\_    *Staff* experiences many types of incentives, recognitions, and rewards.

\_\_\_\_    The *school* has a climate of kindness and encouragement.

\_\_\_\_    Resources needed by students and staff are secured and distributed fairly in the *school*.

\_\_\_\_    TOTAL SCORE

*High Expectations*

\_\_\_\_    *Students* believe that they can succeed.

\_\_\_\_    *Students* experience little or no labeling (formally or informally) or tracking.

\_\_\_\_    *Staff* believes members can succeed.

\_\_\_\_    *Staff* is rewarded for risk taking and excellence (e.g., merit pay).

\_\_\_\_    The *school* provides growth plans for staff and students with clear outcomes, regular reviews, and supportive feedback.

\_\_\_\_    An attitude of "can do" permeates the *school*.

\_\_\_\_    TOTAL SCORE

*Opportunities for Meaningful Participation*

___ *Students* are involved in programs that emphasize service to other students, school, and the community.

___ *Students* are involved in school decision making, including governance and policy.

___ *Staff* is involved in school decision making, including governance and policy.

___ *Staff* is engaged in both job-specific and organization-wide responsibilities.

___ Everyone in the *school* community (students, parents, staff) is viewed as resources rather than problems, objects, or clients.

___ The *school* climate emphasizes "doing what really matters" and risk taking.

___ TOTAL SCORE

___ OVERALL ASSESSMENT SCORE (total of each of the six sections)

Student ___ (total of the first two scores in each section)

Staff ___ (total of the second two scores in each section)

School ___ (total of the last two scores in each section)

Range of scores: overall, 36–144; each section, 6–24; students, staff, and the school, 12–48. Lower scores indicate positive resilience building; higher scores indicate a need for improvement.

# RESOURCE C

## Moving From Risk to Resiliency in Our Schools

### Creating Opportunities to Learn

| From | To |
|------|-----|

### Relationships
### Between and Among Teachers, Students, and Parents

| Hierarchical, blaming, controlling | Characterized by caring, positive expectations and participation |
|------|-----|

### Teacher Behavior and Attitudes

| Conveys message: "This work is required; you may not be able to dot it; you're on your own." Looks for deficiencies | Conveys message: "This work is important; I know you can do it; I won't give up on you." Looks for strengths |
|------|-----|

### Physical Environment

| Peeling paint; boarded windows; dirty; things don't work; graffiti | Painted; clean; works; kids work on display |
|------|-----|

### Curriculum and Instruction

| Fragmented, nonexperiential; Eurocentric focus; limited access to broad variety courses and activities; teaches to narrow range of learning styles; status-quo | Integrated, experience-based/service learning; college core/enrich available to all students; reflects cultures of all students; access to broad variety of courses and activities; teaches to broad range learning styles; critical inquiry |
|------|-----|

## Creating Opportunities to Learn

| From | To |
|---|---|

### Grouping

| | |
|---|---|
| Homogenous; tracking; individual competition; pull-out programs | Heterogeneous; untracked; cooperative groups; inclusive all students; "families" |

### Evaluation

| | |
|---|---|
| Assess only limited range of intelligences; standardized; focus on "right" answers | Assess multiple intelligences; holistic; authentic, portfolio; fosters self-reflection |

### Motivation

| | |
|---|---|
| Competitive; extrinsic rewards; no involvement in meaningful decision making | Collaborating; intrinsic rewards; active engagement—connected to learner's interest, strengths, and real world |

### Responsibility

| | |
|---|---|
| Authority-determined rules; "sage on state"/dictator; no involvement in meaningful decision making | Democratic, consensual; "guide on the side"/facilitator; active participation in decision-making peer helping community service |

# RESOURCE D

## Checklist

Place a • by the items that demonstrate your strengths-based practices.
Place a + by items you would like to improve or strengthen.

### I demonstrate CARING AND SUPPORT for my students by

___ Creating and sustaining a caring sense of community
___ Creating one-to-one connections
___ Actively listening/using eye contact
___ Paying attention and showing interest
___ Praising and encouraging
___ Getting to know hopes, interests, and dreams
___ Showing respect
___ Being nonjudgmental
___ Looking beneath "problem" behavior"
___ Using humor/smiling/laughing
___ Creating small, personalized groups
___ Creating opportunities for peer helping and
     cross-age mentoring

### I communicate HIGH EXPECTATIONS to my students by

___ Believing in the resilient nature of every child
___ Seeing culture as an asset
___ Challenging and supporting ("You can do it; I'll be there to
     help.")
___ Connecting learning to students' interests, strengths, experi-
     ences, dreams, and goals
___ Encouraging creativity and imagination
___ Seeing student behavior as driven by basic needs (love,
     belonging, etc.)
___ Setting clear expectations/boundaries/structure
___ Using rituals and traditions
___ Using a variety of instructional strategies to tap multiple
     intelligences
___ Conveying to students they have power to change and deter-
     mine their own behavior and thoughts

**I provide opportunities for my students' PARTICIPATION AND CONTRIBUTION by**

\_\_\_   Providing opportunities for students to plan, make decisions, and problem solve

\_\_\_   Empowering youth to help create school/classroom rules

**Creating opportunities for creative expression**

\_\_\_   Art

\_\_\_   Music

\_\_\_   Writing/poetry

\_\_\_   Storytelling/drama

**Inviting the active participation of often-excluded groups**

\_\_\_   Girls/women

\_\_\_   Youth of color

\_\_\_   Youth with special needs

\_\_\_   Infusing service learning

\_\_\_   Offering peer helping, cross-age helping, and peer-support groups

\_\_\_   Using cooperative learning

\_\_\_   Providing ongoing opportunities for personal reflection

\_\_\_   Providing ongoing opportunities for dialog/discussion

\_\_\_   Providing ongoing opportunities for experiential/active learning

# RESOURCE E

## RYDMflyer

Are you doing all you can to promote positive development, well-being, and academic success among all youth?

Are youth developing qualities and characteristics associated with positive academic, social, and health outcomes?

How connected are they to school, home, community, and peers?

Do they have caring adults and friends they can count on?

Are they held to high positive expectations and provided with the supports necessary to succeed?

Are they given opportunities to participate in activities that are meaningful, relevant, and engaging, and that foster a sense of responsibility and contribution?

Are you creating environments that
✓ meet fundamental youth needs?
✓ promote academic achievement?
✓ create safe schools?
✓ increase parent involvement?
✓ build community partnerships?

### Find answers in the CHKS Resilience & Youth Development Module!

## RESILIENCE, YOUTH DEVELOPMENT & ASSET ASSESSMENT

Identifying resilience-related youth assets
to promote positive development and school success.

### What is the California Healthy Kids Survey (CHKS)?

θ A state-of-the-art, flexible modular health behavior survey for elementary and secondary school youth that can be used to assess:
  ∞ use of alcohol, tobacco, and other drugs
  ∞ violence, harassment, weapons possession, safety, and suicide
  ∞ nutrition, exercise, and physical health
  ∞ sexual behavior and teen pregnancy
  ∞ resilience and assets

### What is the Resilience & Youth Development Module (RYDM)?

θ A comprehensive, balanced, high-quality assessment of resilience factors and assets that research has consistently associated with positive development, risk behavior protection, and achievement.
  ∞ based on the latest research and theory
  ∞ developmentally appropriate
  ∞ has psychometric reliability and construct validity
θ A short, stand-alone module of the California Healthy Kids Survey for grades 7–12, which can be administered by itself or along with the CHKS Core Module to provide an assessment of essential risk and protective factors.
θ An integrated component of the single elementary CHKS.

### What does the RYDM measure?

θ Eleven environmental assets in the school, home, community, and peer environments.
  ∞ caring relationships
  ∞ high positive and clear expectations
  ∞ opportunities for meaningful participation
θ Six individual assets or resilience factors.
  ∞ cooperation and communication
  ∞ goal orientation
  ∞ problem solving and self-efficacy
  ∞ self-awareness and empathy
θ Youth connectedness to the school, home, community, and peer group.

### Who developed it?

θ Developed by a team of WestEd researchers with over seventeen years of health survey and youth development experience, including Bonnie Benard, internationally recognized resilience authority.
θ Expert assistance provided by a workgroup of youth development, health, and prevention researchers and practitioners.

> *The higher in assets on the CHKS, the lower the risk behaviors and the higher the school achievement!*

### How are the results reported?

- θ Comprehensive reports provide the proportion of youth that measure high, moderate, and low on each asset and total assets. Datasets also available for analysis.
- θ Explanations of the theory and research supporting each asset.
- θ Data showing the relationship of risk behaviors to assets.
- θ Examples of strategies and programs for promoting each external and internal asset.

### How can you use the RYDM?

- θ Determine the level of assets associated with positive social, academic, and health outcomes.
- θ Measure school connectedness and analyze links between youth development and achievement.
- θ Measure whether necessary environmental supports and opportunities are in place.
- θ Raise local awareness and understanding of youth developmental needs and how to meet them.
- θ Promote school-parent-community collaboration.
- θ Monitor success in fostering high asset levels in all youth.
- θ Learn strategies to address identified needs and foster positive development and resilience.

### What do users have to say about the RYDM?

- θ "The RYDM data helped us focus on the positive and measure strengths, rather than highlight negative issues and write policies that punish. It also helped us finally forge meaningful school-community collaboration in prevention planning" (Tom Asward, Contra Costa County).
- θ "The Resilience Module gives me information that I can really use to affect a positive change in the total school environment. Asset building is the way to go in the future to really change students' lives for the better" (Trudy Burrus, Saddleback Valley School District).

## CHKS Resilience & Youth Development Theoretical Framework

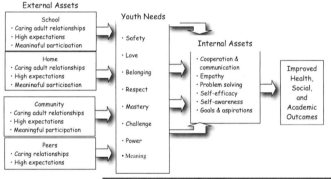

For more information: call toll-free at *888.841.7536*, contact Bonnie Benard at *510.302.4208*, or visit *www.wested.org/hks*. Workshops and training available in resilience theory, program development, and data use.

# RESOURCE F

## Cesar Chavez School
## Written Spring 1998
(This case study was placed in Chapter 3 in the first edition)

*I began seeing a high percentage of our students dropping out when they reached middle school and high school. Their Spanish was bad, and their English worse.*

—Andy Dias, Bilingual Resource Teacher

*Seventy-five percent of our fifth graders were not on grade level. It didn't matter if it was the students in our bilingual or SDAIE (specially designed academic instruction in English) classes. The turnover rate at Chavez is very large. About 54% of our fifth graders were not here in first grade.*

—Ida Larsen, Reading Recovery Resource Teacher

*Our goal is biliteracy for all students. Academics is only a part of it. We really want to see loving people, productive, creative members of society.*

—Andy Dias

## A School Snapshot

I began working with the principal and several teacher leaders in the spring of 1996. We examined the school culture and looked for ways to build a more resilient learning community for students and staff. Teacher-leaders and the principal were passionately committed to improving the literacy of their students. Their single-minded focus impressed me.

The teacher-leaders asked me to spend time at the school trying to understand why student outcomes were not improving more rapidly. Most teachers had been attending a variety of literacy trainings, and discussions in the faculty room and in staff meetings often focused on implementing the strategies taught in the trainings. After talking with many staff members and observing in classrooms, I suggested that there was little coherence to what teachers were doing. Almost all teachers were trying to implement new literacy strategies. However, each teacher was doing it in his or her own way. There was little coordination, no peer and expert coaching, and no accountability system in place to support the implementation of new teaching strategies.

They decided to address these issues with the full faculty at an upcoming professional development day. As a result of their facilitation, all faculty

- agreed on five reading and four writing best practices;
- agreed to focus instruction on these best practices;
- using their lesson plan books for the previous two weeks, listed activities they had implemented that fit under each of the best practices;
- highlighted which best practices they felt most competent with and which they felt least competent with;
- paired off with another teacher who felt competent in areas the other teacher felt less competent in;
- agreed to peer coach with the second teacher, with a focus on the strategies highlighted.

I attended a faculty meeting the following week and introduced the staff to peer coaching, including several role play situations. The next week every teacher was given release time in order to peer coach and to be peer coached, including preconference, classroom observations, and postconference. During the subsequent week, I attended a second faculty meeting in order to give the faculty an opportunity to talk about the peer coaching experience, role play the pre and postconferences, and set an agenda for peer coaching for the next school year.

## Background Information

Cesar Chavez School is located in one of the poorest neighborhoods in east San Jose. The school enrollment is 836—84 percent Hispanic, 11 percent Asian, 3 percent white, not Hispanic, 2 percent other. Sixty-five percent of the students are English language learning students. Ninety-one percent receive free or reduced price lunches.

Due to substantial enrollment growth (666 in 1996–1997 to 836 in 1997–1998) and the California Class Size Reduction

Program, Chavez hired six new teachers in January 1997 and eleven new teachers for 1997–1998. Thus, at the beginning of 1997–1998, seventeen of the forty teachers were new to Chavez. In addition, the principal resigned during the summer of 1997, and the Title VII coordinator was appointed to be the new principal.

In fall 1997 the new Alum Rock superintendent told each school to adopt a formal literacy program and make it the focus of their school literacy plan. Schools did not all need to choose the same program. The Cesar Chavez faculty decided, with superintendent approval, to focus their plan on the nine literacy strategies rather than adopting a formal literacy program. Through a competitive, in-district grant program, Chavez was one of five Alum Rock schools awarded $88,000 to support implementation. The money was used to hire a part-time teacher to work with kindergarten students who were limited in both their primary and secondary languages, a part-time teacher to work through the school parent center to offer parenting and ESL classes, and a teacher to work with fourth and fifth graders who were below grade level in English reading. Money was also used to purchase books and printers to support instruction. In addition, Chavez received a grant of $50,000 from the Community Foundation to support literacy and money from the Noyce Foundation to train two teachers to be reading recovery teachers.

Several important components of their literacy plan were already in place. There were four reading recovery teachers to work with primary grade students as a safety net. Considerable money had been used to purchase instructional materials. Also, the Parent Institute for Quality Education had conducted twelve-week parent education classes twice in the previous year, enrolling over two hundred Chavez parents.

Staff members say that 1995–1997 was spent learning literacy strategies and purchasing appropriate instructional materials; 1997–1998 was the year to build in the necessary support to assure implementation.

## A School Snapshot

Throughout the 1997–1998 school year, fifteen teachers, Grades K–3, participated in an Early Literacy Inservice Course (ELIC) taught by one of the Chavez teachers and funded by the school district. In addition to serving as the instructor, this teacher worked with each of the fifteen teachers as an expert coach and demonstration teacher. The fifteen teachers were a mix of new and experienced staff. In addition, seven non-ELIC teachers, one paraprofessional, and the principal attended another early literacy program, California Early Literacy Learning (CELL). And, three other teachers were receiving the very intensive reading recovery training. Thus twenty-seven staff members were involved in literacy training.

In January 1998 the staff was surveyed to learn if the nine literacy strategies were being used consistently by teachers. Responses indicated that implementation was inconsistent for many teachers. I was asked to return to the school to meet with three teacher leaders and the principal. We agreed that (1) additional peer coaching training and support were necessary, (2) peer coaching should focus on the strategies most appropriate at particular grade levels, (3) the leadership team needed to take on the role of "cheer leading squad," encouraging and reinforcing teachers as they implemented literacy strategies and as they peer coached, and (4) a system needed to be put in place so that the principal could more easily monitor implementation of the strategies. From January to May, I met with the staff four times to facilitate peer coaching. On a voluntary basis, most of the staff paired off and conducted peer coaching cycles during the winter and spring.

As a part of our planning, the school leadership team and principal agreed that an accountability system was necessary. All teachers were suppose to do an "alternative ranking" of their students based on running records three times per year. This was turned into the principal. They were also to use this information to meet in grade-level teams to plan support for all targeted students. The leadership team developed a form to support this process, and the principal agreed to hold teachers accountable for implementing the grade-level literacy strategies, conducting the running records, and developing and implementing a plan for each targeted student. Baseline data, using running records of district/school benchmark books, for all grades was established in February 1998.

## Uniqueness of the School

What happens for a staff when they accept the collaborative responsibility to help every student be literate and to create a resilient learning community that supports students and teachers in this effort? I have visited Cesar Chavez many times. I have talked with teachers and students. I have walked and driven through the neighborhood. If the staff at Chavez did not foster resilience for each other, I do not know how they could come to work every day and care so deeply about children whose needs are so great.

Below I intersperse a few of my observations with many quotes I have gathered from conversations with Chavez teachers.

*Collegiality*

> "This is my second year as a teacher. There is a very apparent and deep commitment amongst the veteran teachers to the literacy of kids. They are the models for what is expected of the newer teachers. This commitment and support from other teachers and administrators really makes a difference for me. They think nothing of providing suggestions, ideas, materials, and support—anything I might need to facilitate lessons and to accomplish my job as best as I can."

> "We are good friends at this school. Many of us earned our bilingual credentials together in college and were hired together. Unlike my husband who also teaches, the people I work with are my friends who I call on the weekend."

> "When I came to this school from another district, I got a lot of support from other teachers. Teachers at Chavez support each other and are focused in a common direction. There is none of the bickering that occurred at my previous school."

Anytime I have visited Chavez, whether I sit in the faculty room, the office, staff meetings, or school leadership team meetings, I am impressed by the positive talk about students and by the support, laughter, and joy these teachers find in working together.

*Intellectual Stimulation*

> "One of the things that makes the profession attractive to me is that I've had plenty of opportunities for professional development. I like going to school, and I value the opportunity to learn in order to benefit my students and me. I've been teaching for twenty-seven years, and I still get involved in school leadership and in student study teams so that I get information that I can use with my kids."

"One of the reasons we have that sense of professionalism is that, even before we developed site-based leadership, José encouraged teachers to attend whatever conferences they requested."

"Not a lot of teachers leave at 2:45. Twenty-one of the teachers have taken the whole year course in effective first teaching. Fifteen are currently enrolled in ELIC. There is an amazing commitment by teachers here."

Recently, I was at Chavez facilitating peer-coaching training with the staff. I asked Andy Dias to observe how long it took for the staff to actively engage in the small-group simulation I set up for them. Often, at the end of the school day, teachers need prompting to begin serious work. Andy's observation was that all teachers were in their groups and on task within one minute. This is consistent with my observations over time. This staff takes professional development very seriously. Clearly, the number of teachers who voluntarily participate in the variety of literacy trainings is indicative of this commitment.

*Respect*

"We give each other room to vent and to understand each other's positions. It is the unwritten law at Chavez that we respect each other, work through issues in grade level meetings, and not butt heads."

"We have worked very hard to not have friction between lower and upper grades or between bilingual and SDAIE teachers. The leadership team has to make decisions for the whole school. We have gotten away from thinking only about our kids in our own classrooms and instead think about the kids in the school as all of our kids. We team-teach; we switch kids around; we share lessons and materials; we plan lessons together."

"It helps that we each have eight hours of paid time for grade-level planning outside of school hours."

"We've always had a united staff. Regardless of who the administrator was, the staff was a constant factor. Teachers either like it or they don't. The majority have stayed. And we stay in contact with those people who have left and gone on to bigger and better things. We invite them back for showers and staff parties, and they come."

"Until last year when we went to twenty to one, we have always had teachers with the appropriate credentials. All of the bilingual teachers were fully certified. This was very unusual and was important to our sense of professionalism."

I hear the same message from teachers at Chavez that I hear at Rosemary, "These kids need me. They appreciate me and tell me so. Their parents are so appreciative. What I do every day is important."

*Voice*

"We have had five principals in the last six years, and the school has kept running itself. Schools need strong leaders, but it is better when there is strong school leadership that includes the principal, as it is now at Chavez."

"Site-based management empowers teachers since we feel we are making decisions that affect students. As we make budget decisions, we build in support and resources where we see the need."

"Since we support each other, people are not afraid to get in and work. Work is not the problem. It is being able to have the materials and skills to do it."

Under the leadership of former principal José Garcia, who left during the summer of 1997, and current principal Eva Ruth, formerly the bilingual resource teacher at the school and coordinator of the Title VII grant, the teacher leadership team has a major voice in school decision making. They meet at least twice a month. This leadership team, consisting of about nine teachers and the principal, is responsible for making many of the most important decisions facing the school. Members of this team set the school plan, and oversee the school budget. It is the teacher-leaders who take issues to the staff at large for input and for their consensus.

*Increased Job Satisfaction*

"You must have love for teaching based on love for the kids. I've been at Chavez for twenty-eight years, and I can tell you that if you have that love, the rest is easy."

"What attracted me to this school are the kids. They are lively and full of life. You can inspire and motivate them, open the world to them."

"As an adult in the community, I see the need for every student to be literate and to think critically and analytically. The challenges they face are difficult enough that if they don't have the skills they might not make the right decisions. . . . I entered the profession for political reasons. I've always had strong feelings about minority children not doing as well in school and why. I feel that the best possible way for me to contribute at this point in my life is in the classroom. Having a male teacher may serve as a model to not follow certain paths. I hope that I offer them an alternative, especially for so many that do not have dads at home. That is, in fact, who I am for many of my students. Just now, as I walked past the cafeteria and saw all the kids sitting together, I was reminded of why I'm doing this."

It is this love for children and deep caring for the future of these children that makes Cesar Chavez such a special place. When children come from communities pervaded with poverty, the protective factors that foster resilience must be at the heart of the school if the children are to have a hopeful future.

*Overcoming the Obstacles*

"The children are so very needy, not only academically but also in their social life and in the community. We get them for only a few hours a day, but we try to make this a safe place for them, a place where they feel comfortable, a sanctuary where they can forget what is happening at home and in the community. We want them to feel safe, wanted and loved."

I know of no school staff that exudes more of an infectious and deeply held commitment to each and every student. The school has grown large; the number of new teachers needing support is overwhelming; there is never enough time. However, the staff clearly knows that improving the literacy of the students they serve cannot be solved with a magic wand. They have been consistent in saying to the district that professional development must stay focused on literacy for at least three to five years and that resources must be focused in this direction.

## Student Outcomes

- **Apprenda** (norm referenced test given in Spanish)
  Total reading scores for 1997 were substantially higher than for 1996 in Grades one, two, four, and five. For Grades two, four, and five the student average scores were above the 45th percentile. Total language scores were also higher for students in those grades. For Grades two and four, the student average scores were above the 50th percentile.

- **Stanford Achievement Test** (norm referenced test given in English)
  Scores were not as impressive when students take the tests in English. For all grade levels, the student averages for both total reading and total language were in the 20th and low 30th percentiles.

As stated earlier, 1997–1998 is seen by staff as the first year of implementing the literacy strategies they have spent the 1995–1998 years learning. We know that it takes three to seven years to successfully implement a quality literacy program. Apprenda results lead me to be optimistic that over the next few years, student literacy at Cesar Chavez will improve substantially.

# References

Agee, J., & Evans, W. (1960). *Let us now praise famous men.* Cambridge, MA: Riverside Press.

Barnett, D., McKowen, C., & Bloom, G. (1998). A school without a principal. *Educational Leadership, 55*(7), 48–49.

Barth, R. (1991). *Improving schools from within: Teachers, parents, and principals can make a difference.* San Francisco: Jossey-Bass.

Benard, B. (1991). *Fostering resiliency in kids: Protective factors in the family, school, and community.* Portland, OR: Western Center for Drug-Free Schools and Communities.

Benard, B. (1993). Fostering resiliency in kids. *Educational Leadership, 51*(3), 44–48.

Benard, B. (1995). *Fostering resilience in children.* Urbana, IL: ERIC.

Benard, B. (2003). Turnaround teachers and schools. In B. Williams (Ed.), *Closing the achievement gap: A vision for changing beliefs and practices.* Alexandria, VA: Association for Supervision and Curriculum Development.

Bridges, W. (1991). *Managing transitions: Making the most of change.* Reading, MA: Addison-Wesley.

Burns, T., & Lofquist, B. (1996). *The next step: Integrating resiliency and community development in the school.* Tucson, AZ: Development Publications.

Butler, K. (1997, March/April). The anatomy of resilience. *Networker,* 22–31.

Chaleff, I. (1995). *The courageous follower: Standing up to and for our leaders.* San Francisco: Berrett-Koehler Publishers.

Cotton, K. (1996). *School size, school climate, and student performance: Close-up #20.* Portland, OR: Northwest Regional Educational Laboratory.

Cummins, J. (1996). *Negotiating identities: Education for empowerment in a diverse society.* Ontario, CA: California Association for Bilingual Education.

Cushman, K. (1995). Making the good school better: The essential question of rigor. *Horace, 11*(4).

Darling-Hammond, L. (1997). *The right to learn: A blueprint for creating schools that work.* San Francisco: Jossey-Bass.

Deiro, J. (2005). *Teachers do make a difference: The teacher's guide to connecting with students.* Thousand Oaks, CA: Corwin Press.

Evans, R. (1996). *The human side of school change.* San Francisco: Josey-Bass.

Fullan, M. (1998). Leadership for the twenty-first century: Breaking the bonds of dependency. *Educational Leadership, 55*(7), 6–11.

Hanson, T., Austin, G., & Lee-Bayha, J. (2004). *How are student health risks & resilience related to the academic progress of schools? Ensuring that no child is left behind.* San Francisco: WestEd.

Henderson, N., & Milstein, M. M. (1996). *Resiliency in schools: Making it happen for students and educators.* Thousand Oaks, CA: Corwin Press.

Henze, R., Katz, A., Norte, E., Sather, S. E., & Walker, E. (2002). *Leading for diversity: How school leaders promote positive interethnic relations.* Thousand Oaks, CA: Corwin Press.

Katzenmeyer, M., & Moller, G. (2001). *Awakening the sleeping giant: Helping teachers develop as leaders.* Thousand Oaks, CA: Corwin Press.

Kitashima, M. (1997). The faces of resiliency: Lessons from my life: no more "children at risk" . . . all children are "at promise." *Resiliency in Action, 2*(3), 30–36.

Klonsky, M. (1996). *Small schools: The numbers tell a story.* Chicago: University of Illinois at Chicago.

Krovetz, M. L., & Arriaza, G. (2006). *Collaborative teacher leadership: How teachers can foster equitable schools.* Thousand Oaks, CA: Corwin Press.

Krovetz, M. L., & Cohick, D. (1993). Professional collegiality can lead to school change. *Kappan, 75,* 331–333.

Lambert, L. (2003). *Leadership capacity for lasting school improvement.* Alexandria, VA: Association for Supervision and Curriculum Development.

Lindsay, R., Robins, K. N., & Terrell, R. D. (2003). *Cultural proficiency: A manual for schools leaders* (2nd ed.). Thousand Oaks, CA: Corwin Press.

Luthar, S. S. (2000). The construct of resilience: A critical evaluation and guidelines for future research. *Child Development, 71*(3), 543–562.

Marzano, R. J. (2003). *What works in schools: Translating research into action.* Alexandria, VA: Association for Supervision and Curriculum Development.

McTighe, J., & Wiggins, G. (2004). *Understanding by Design: Professional development handbook.* Alexandria, VA: Association for Supervision and Curriculum Development.

Meier, D. (1995). *The power of their ideas.* Boston: Beacon Press.

Nieto, S. (1996). *Affirming diversity: The sociopolitical context of multicultural education.* New York: Longman.

Noddings, N. (1995). A morally defensible mission for schools in the 21st century. *Kappan, 76*(5), 365–368.

Poplin, M., & Weeres, J. (1994). *Voices from the inside: A report on schooling from inside the classroom.* Claremont, CA: The Institute for Education in Transformation.

Powell, A. G., Farrar, E., & Cohen, D. K. (1985). *The shopping mall high school: Winners and losers in the educational marketplace.* Boston: Houghton Mifflin.

Rutter, M. (1979). *Fifteen thousand hours: Secondary schools and their effects on children.* Cambridge, MA: Harvard University Press.

Sagor, R. (1993). *How to conduct collaborative action research.* Alexandria, VA: Association for Supervision and Curriculum Development.

Sarason, S. (1990). *The predictable failure of educational reform.* San Francisco: Josey-Bass.

Singleton, G. (2006). *Courageous conversations about race: A field guide for achieving equity in schools.* Thousand Oaks, CA: Corwin Press.

Sizer, T. R. (1985). *Horace's compromise.* Boston: Houghton Mifflin.

Sizer, T. R. (1992). *Horace's school.* Boston: Houghton Mifflin.

Sizer, T. R. (1996). *Horace's hope.* Boston: Houghton Mifflin.

Speck, M., & Knipe, C. (2005). *Why can't we get it right?* Thousand Oaks, CA: Corwin Press.

Speck, M., & Krovetz, M. L. (1995). Student resiliency: Building caring learning communities. *Multicultures. 1,* 113–123.

Tomlinson, C. A., & McTighe, J. (2006). *Integrating differentiated instruction and Understanding by Design.* Alexandria, VA: Association for Supervision and Curriculum Development.

Topf, R., Maiwald, V., & Krovetz, M. (2004). Developing resilient learning communities to close the achievement gap. In H. Waxman, Y. Padron, & J. Gray (Eds.), *Educational resiliency: Students, teacher, and school perspective* (pp. 205–226). Greenwich, CT: Information Age.

Wasley, P., & Lear, R. (2001, March). Small schools, real gains. *Educational Leadership, 58*, (6), 22–27.

Waxman, H., Padron, Y., & Gray, J. (Eds.). (2004). *Educational resiliency: Students, teacher, and school perspective.* Greenwich, CT: Information Age.

Weissbourd, R. (1996). *The vulnerable child: What really hurts America's children and what we can do about it.* Reading, MA: Addison Wesley.

Werner, E. (1996). How children become resilient: Observations and cautions. *Resiliency in Action, 1*(1), 18–28.

Werner, E., & Smith, R. S. (1992). *Overcoming the odds: High risk children from birth to adulthood.* Ithaca, NY: Cornell University Press.

Wiggins, G. & McTighe, J. (1998). *Understanding by Design.* Alexandria, VA: Association for Supervision and Curriculum Development.

# INDEX